BREAKPOINTS

BREAKPOINTS

MAKING CAREER STAGES WORK FOR YOU

by Andrew Sherwood

Doubleday & Company, Inc., Garden City, New York
1986

Library of Congress Cataloging-in-Publication Data

Sherwood, Andrew.
  Breakpoints: making career stages work for you.

  Includes index.
  1. Vocational guidance. I. Veley, Charles, 1943– . II. Title.
HF5381.S547 1986   331.7'02

ISBN 0-385-19952-X
Library of Congress Catalog Card Number 85-20602

Acknowledgments

Every book requires teamwork, but *Breakpoints* is perhaps more the result of teamwork than most. It's the result of creative collaboration with the wonderful professional staff of the Goodrich & Sherwood Company, a happy association that's spanned the better part of two decades and was in full swing long before we decided to put the *Breakpoints* concepts on paper and into print.

This gratitude extends beyond the day-to-day professional collaboration the G&S staff and I have enjoyed, however. Once the decision was made to put our *Breakpoints* concepts into book form, the formidable tasks began. We had to organize what had become second nature to many of us in the course of our normal everyday activity. Our professional staff gave generously of their time and experience both in initial data-gathering interviews and in later, follow-up consultation. My only regret is that because of our limitation on space and subject matter, we were not able to include all the high-quality data and anecdotes that the G&S staff provided; however, there is consolation in the thought that we've gathered enough material for another book.

My thanks go also to the thousands of clients, both corporate and individual, who've come to Goodrich & Sherwood over the years. Their experiences, of course, are our experiences, and the ideas we present in *Breakpoints* are based on thousands of individual career stories, ranging across all levels of management in companies from those closely held through the Fortune 500. The names of some of our client companies, and the names of other companies we've encountered, are reproduced in many of the anecdotes presented here. But to protect the privacy of our individual clients, we have, in most cases, altered names, locations, industry types, personal circumstances, and even quoted dialogue to prevent recognition. Remaining in all the anecdotes, however, are underlying principles our professional staff has distilled from these thousands and thousands of career encounters. I'm grateful for the opportunity we've all had to work together.

In particular, I would like to thank the following Goodrich & Sherwood people and others who were invaluable to the creation of this book:

Jane C. Antil
Frederick W. Ball
Charles F. Bischoff, Jr.
James F. Blair
Henry L. Collins, III
Paul Conboy
Mary Ellen Curley
Theodore V. Fowler, Sr.
Jack F. Gow
William H. Heald
Stanley C. Johnson
Sally S. Keane
Robert L. Laud
Carole S. Lieberman
Debbie Lipton
James D. Mead
Thomas W. C. Miller
Richard A. Miners
Frank R. Palma
Gail A. Petersen
Edmund Piccolino
Barbara Pickens

Deborah A. Pontosky
Marcia P. Pryde
Celeste P. Rachell
Saul G. Samet
Lawrence Sands
Michael R. Scanlon
Thomas G. Schmitt
Jennifer E. Siegel
Walter O. Sonyi
Richard E. Spann
L. Marshall Stellfox
Linford E. Stiles
T. Allen Swann
Leo L. Tonner
Joyce A. Varady
Charles Veley
Muriel R. Vogel
Proctor S. Waterman
Kathryn Wolf
Lee Wotherspoon
Adrian Zackheim

CONTENTS

FOREWORD:
Why This Book?

Be honest. How many of you chose your present career position by some logical, rational means? How many of you even chose your college, your major, or your first job by some logical, rational means? Did you go to Buckmore University because the course of study fit your aptitude profile or matched your long-term career goals? If you did, you're a rare product of the education process as it is generally structured.

Most likely, unless you were indeed fortunate and most unusual, neither you nor anyone else ever gave sustained thought to your career. If you're like most people, the only analysis went something like: "You're good with numbers, so why not consider a career in engineering or data processing or, say, accounting?" Odds are that you shuddered and escaped the discussion at your earliest opportunity. And, if you're working today, the odds are that you *still* haven't given serious effort to organizing your career.

The plain truth is that most people don't—or can't—give you good career advice. In the business world, they're wrestling with their own unplanned careers. And in academia, teacher goals dictate that you regurgitate Accounting 101 or Sociology 104, rather than to plan where you'll go from there. Even with all the books and counseling proffered up during the previous thirty years, something still isn't working.

Our business at Goodrich & Sherwood tells us the problem begins with the educational system, which turns out millions of men and women each year who have little or no idea what they are trained for, would be best suited for, or would like to do. What happens to them?

They may leave the campus with a job—courtesy of campus recruiting sharks who do little to address career questions. Or they may go home jobless. If they do rejoin the family, the pressure soon begins to build. "When are you going to get a job? What are your friends doing?" Or worse: "What about the great job Johnny Smith got with Sears?" Sound familiar?

Parents who expected a package all gift-wrapped, ready to go to work, now face lurking fears of a permanently unemployed deadbeat who, if not on the government unemployment lines, is certainly on theirs. Tension mounts.

So what happens next? Ne'er-do-well takes job. Any job. The best job to be found. Career choice, planning, etc., are forgotten. Now everyone is happy and proud and—a career is launched.

Someday I hope there'll be a revolution and the education system will modify itself—albeit at gunpoint—to a more efficient career goal oriented process. But for now, folks, this is it. Is it any wonder that when we meet people in their forties, fifties, or sixties, they still ask, "What do I really want to do?"

We've created this book partly to help you answer this question for yourself, because no one else will. Just as important, we've created this book to help you achieve your career goal once you've identified it, and to avoid the career troubles we've seen so many talented but unwary people encounter.

Whether you're a student just beginning a career, an executive in the middle of your career, or a retiree planning a new future, we hope you'll gain some wisdom from our experience and observations.

BREAKPOINTS

Chapter 1

Capsule Summary
The Story of BREAKPOINTS

Every career has different stages.

Each stage has a powerful effect on the way you work, and on the way others *allow* you to work.

The influence of these stages is far greater than most people realize. If you understand how they affect you, you can eliminate the hidden cause of many problems you've blamed on stress, on overwork, on a personality conflict with your supervisor, or even on your marriage. When you see your own career path and direct your own progress toward the stage that's right for you, you may come to see that many of the emotional strains you've been under were really just the superficial symptoms of a career-stage mismatch.

But to make the right moves from one career stage to the next, you must first understand the concept of "breakpoints." At Goodrich & Sherwood, the nation's largest full-service human resources consulting company, we developed this concept through the experiences of nearly two decades. Working with America's largest corporations to help executives make their careers more productive, we found certain recurring career patterns that seemed to have a force of their own. At certain points, these patterns of events seemed to "take control," moving people into career problems or new opportunities whether those people wanted to move or not.

Most people are taken by surprise by the suddenness of these changes. It's a bit like paddling a small canoe down a large river. Most of the trip is quiet in a slow current. As the river narrows, the current picks up, things begin to happen quickly and it is here that you encounter rapids and rocks. In planning your career and on the river, the key is to use your quiet time to become prepared for the future. Most people wait until they're in the rapids and make poor, hurried choices.

BREAKPOINTS will show you how to prepare. We've come to realize that people need help in recognizing these points of sudden change, to understand how career stages can affect them. Just as important, people need help to understand how they can take control of their career plans to actively shape the future. Unless these key concepts are mastered and made a part of a longer-term career plan, job-hunting ideas or techniques are temporary patches rather than long-term strategy. Such techniques can *hold back* your progress, sidetracking you into a job that doesn't fit your career or personal goals.

BREAKPOINTS is not a book about job hunting, and though the stories of G&S clients may help you if you embark on a job-hunting campaign, that's not our purpose in writing this book.

Instead, BREAKPOINTS helps you put your present job into logical perspective. It will help you understand, possibly for the first time, how your career fits, or should fit, into your life plan.

It will help you determine what career stage you're at now, and how that stage is affecting you.

It can help you discover career needs and goals that, up till now, have been a hidden part of your personal makeup.

It will help you chart your future course toward the career stage that's right for you.

It will show you how to recognize "breakpoint" conditions indicating that you're on the verge of a career move—whether you know it or not.

It will identify "breakpoint" danger spots and direct you to take advantage of "breakpoint" opportunities.

How do we propose to do all this?

First, we're going to show you what a career looks like—how you move from one stage to the next and encounter different problems and opportunities at each stage.

Second, we're going to help you test yourself, to determine your ultimate career goal, and to create the career chart that shows the steps you'll take to reach that goal.

Third, we're going to identify those key moments of transition, the "breakpoints" that you're likely to encounter throughout your career.

Some of these breakpoints we call "universal"—you can encounter them regardless of which career stage you happen to be in at the time. We'll show you their *Breakpoint Signals*—those signs and events that indicate you're at a particular breakpoint. We'll explain the *Breakpoint Forces:* those underlying powers in the business world and in the dynamics of the human spirit that you need to understand in order to make each breakpoint work in your favor. Then we'll give you our *Breakpoint Strategy:* the tactics and techniques we've found most successful in dealing with each of these career "moments of truth."

Fourth, we'll describe in separate chapters the "special" breakpoints that apply to each of the specific career stages that you'll encounter. For each stage, we discuss the *Performance Breakpoints:* those critical moments during each career phase when facets of your work become key to your career progress. We include as well *Personal Breakpoints:* those times during each career stage when what's going on in your personal relationships and personal emotions can most frequently affect your career. And, since our experience at G&S has shown that a major factor in your success at work will be the relationships you are able to form with your superiors, subordinates, and co-workers, we include *Political Breakpoints* for each career phase. For each of these breakpoints, we'll describe the *Breakpoint Signals* that should alert you to the career "rapids" ahead, the *Breakpoint Forces* at work, and the *Breakpoint Strategy* we recommend.

Since our experience shows that career success for the married person is strongly influenced by the husband-wife relationship, we include in these chapters checklists for spouses, showing how husbands and wives can best help the other during each career stage.

Finally, since we know that not all our readers share the same backgrounds, we include "Special Pointers" to cover those situations where background differences may call for you to make specific adjustments.

BREAKPOINTS is for everyone with a career. If you have doubts, as most people do, that you're really "getting somewhere," or if you occasionally suspect that you're missing key career opportunities, you'll find that BREAKPOINTS speaks to your needs. If you've wondered about what it means to be a success—not on someone else's terms but on your own—BREAKPOINTS will show you how to develop your own answers.

Once you've set out your career goals clearly, BREAKPOINTS will show you how to take—and keep—control as you move forward. Using methods G&S has tested and proven with thousands of clients, BREAKPOINTS will help you move to the career stage that's right for you.

Chapter 2

Case in Point

Why BREAKPOINTS *Can Make or Break You*

Once there were two men with similar backgrounds. Both had good business school degrees. Both came out of the military at the same rank. Both took similar marketing jobs at a major national company, in consumer products. At the time our story begins, both were brand managers.

One man, we'll call him Buddy, was brand manager of a product that had been a nationwide hit for decades. Sales were great. Distribution was great. He received good performance reports. His job practically ran itself. Life was smooth and easy. As long as he didn't rock the boat, he saw clear sailing ahead.

The other man we'll call Ed. The company had stuck him with some now-forgotten product we'll call Regal Sceptre. Whatever it was, Regal Sceptre wasn't making it. Ed's product performance reports were down. Distribution was down. Cash flow was down. And so was Ed. He was ready to quit, but then he had an idea.

He marched into his boss's office and tactfully stated that Regal Sceptre was a loser, and that, while Ed wasn't about to stop trying to make it work, he was *bored* presiding over the product's demise. His request? An additional assignment, a special project he could take on the side, to show what he could do and, give him something to work for.

The boss listened to Ed's idea, and gave him an additional product to manage. It didn't have a name. Likely the boss grinned to himself as he made the new assignment, because the product was one nobody had much confidence in. Even Regal Sceptre looked good compared to this stuff. It was some strange idea, some new kind of washing product called a "synthetic detergent."

The story is legend because the synthetic detergent became a nationwide best-seller that's still a hit today. Ed rose from that spare-time assignment to become his company's chairman of the board.

And Buddy? He stayed with the company too. He retired as a mid-level manager, near the same spot that Ed's boss had held. Was he a success? That depends how you measure success, of course. In terms of personal ambitions, however, he didn't reach the career point he wanted to attain.

Ed did.

The Hidden Breakpoint Signal. In hindsight, it's easy to spot Buddy's problem. He was at a breakpoint at the same time Ed was, only he didn't know it. Ed was the luckier of the two, for his frustration with Regal Sceptre forced him to make a move on his own, to take control of his career situation before his career took control of him.

What was Buddy's breakpoint? In Chapter 4, you'll see it labeled as a "Skills Quotient Change," a way of saying that Buddy had become too comfortable on the job. The career trap he fell into we call "the forgotten man." His product was so good *it* was getting the headlines. And since Buddy hadn't *initiated* his product's success story, he couldn't make a name for himself staying where he was.

Unfortunately Buddy was a hard worker, with real ability. His career error was to go with the flow of the business. He kept his nose to the grindstone and did his job, and waited for the company to do the rest. After all, he'd been promoted in school when he'd worked hard and done his assignments. The same would hold true in business, right? Wrong.

Many working people still don't realize how unrealistic this expectation is. Work isn't like school. No matter what you've been led to believe, your bosses aren't in business to groom you for bigger and better things. They're in business to make a profit. It's up to you to make your own way, to achieve your own goals within the profit-making framework. Sometimes what the company wants you to do can be a dead-wrong, worst-case career alternative. But unless you think for yourself and evaluate all the career possibilities at work, you will not realize the disaster your company's getting you into—until it's too late.

Step one to utilizing BREAKPOINTS is to take charge of your own future. To do this intelligently, you'll need to understand what a career is, and how to evaluate your choices. You'll find the information to help you make this evaluation in the next three chapters. After that, we'll sensitize you to breakpoints you'll encounter and show you how to negotiate their challenges and opportunities as you make the most of your career.

Chapter 3

The Career Chart
How to Use This Book

When graduation time rolled around, twenty-seven-year-old Mike landed a job his classmates envied. As financial analyst for a newly formed suburban real estate syndications firm, Mike knew he'd have far more responsibility—and opportunity—than the typical business school graduate.

Mike was confident. He had the skills, the discipline, and he'd been top in his M.B.A. class in the sophisticated techniques the job required. He brought his own IBM PC into the office, and within a week he was turning out thick, number-crunching reports. Though the three principals of the firm seemed unimpressed, Mike kept at it. He knew his techniques were right. When his recommendations were challenged, he stuck to his guns, knowing that many of his reports were nothing short of brilliant.

Six months later, Mike was stunned to learn he was being replaced.

What went wrong? Looking back, Mike says, the mistake is easy to spot. "I made the classic error. I tried to bowl 'em over. People just don't let you do that when you're a rookie."

Did you recognize Mike's problem? It's fairly common. Most people instinctively sense, when they're starting a job, that they shouldn't act as if they know all the answers—even if they *do* know all the answers. People who've been around—at the company or "in the business" for a number of years—have paid their dues. They've worked their way up, often by trial and error, and they're not about to allow a newcomer to treat their experience lightly.

Whether rational or not, this is how human nature affects the system.

When you're in a trainee career phase, you've got to work to the expectations of others. These expectations can limit talent, brilliant though it may be.

The limiting expectations for the trainee phase go beyond demands that you show deference to the experience of your elders. Two other incidents come to mind that illustrate additional trainee limitations.

A number of years ago, I met a bright, young, well-dressed woman we'll call Marilyn, who was a management trainee at Allstate Insurance Co. She told me of her plans to leave the company because of an experience she'd had. She had worked very hard in her first assignment, in fact spending most of her evenings and weekends on the job. One weekend she decided to take a partial break and visit friends. Upon returning on either a Saturday or a Sunday, I don't recall which, she went directly from the airport to the office to get things prepared for the next week's work. She was casually attired, wearing expensive slacks, a blouse, and a blazer. She spent several hours on the job and went home feeling comfortable that she had gotten a good jump on the week.

On Monday, she was surprised to receive a call from her manager, who suggested that when she came to work, she should be properly attired.

"Properly attired—" Yet what struck me first about Marilyn was how well groomed and dressed she *was*. She had been raised on a farm in Indiana and, not wanting to be viewed as an unsophisticated farm girl, was extremely conscious of her appearance. She was also smart and well spoken—all in all, a very together person. Where had she fallen short? She had missed a culture signal, an unwritten "dress code" for trainees at Allstate, and had been dressing *too* well. So doing, she had given her somewhat less well-dressed boss an opening for a criticism he'd wanted to make for some time.

Another trainee limitation is illustrated by what happened to a first-year associate at a major New York law firm, a young man whose capacity for work efficiency later became legendary. As others toiled away evenings and weekends, John would finish his work during normal hours (sometimes early) and leave the office. After a few weeks, resentment grew, for everyone knew that as a first-year associate at the firm you worked long hours. After several months, John was told that in spite of his excellent performance, he would need to spend more time on the job. It just wasn't good for morale for him to be leaving at 5 P.M. John, hurt and confused, left the firm. His lesson, he told me, was that he had misread the culture. He was looking for a position where he could balance his work and lifestyle, while at the firm, the first few years demanded total commitment to the business.

Just as the trainee phase has its own special den.ands, so does each of the other career phases you'll encounter. You'll find a more inclusive discussion of the special problems of the trainee in Chapter 7, which we've devoted exclusively to the trainee level. At this point, however, we want to introduce the other career stages, and get you started on preparing your own career chart.

The career stage you enter after you've successfully concluded your trainee period we call the Initial Responsibility stage or "the Young Turk." In this phase, you're trusted more and your work is reviewed less before it goes "outside." This phase has its own problems, and "powers" to "keep you in your place."

I recall a young second-year brand assistant at the Procter and Gamble company who came to me complaining that he felt hamstrung. He had begun brand work under a "progressive" boss on a small brand in the toilet goods division. The open management style of his first boss gave him great confidence, and he pushed hard for a new assignment on a larger, more prestigious and dynamic brand. In short order, his wish was granted and he found himself on Crest, one of the largest brands in the company.

Now he was working for a new brand manager with a different style and set of needs. The greater freedom and influence he'd expected to have working with a larger brand never materialized. Instead, suddenly he was being ordered to forget his new ideas, keep his head down, and do what he was told.

At another company, the very need to give him these orders could have been the end of the line. Fortunately, this was P&G. He hung on until the next step in the cycle clicked in and he was whisked off to sales training.

What had he—painfully—learned? While individual autonomy may be granted to some degree, the rules of the game vary from boss to boss and from project to project. He mistakenly interpreted the beneficence of his first boss as the rule of the day at P&G. Then he got a rude awakening about his true status with the company.

You must earn your stripes with each work assignment and understand that what works on one assignment may not work on another. Top management takes more interest in the big brands. While working on a leading product may not necessarily get you more personal exposure to the big guns, it will most likely provide more restrictions and control from above.

The larger the business, the more critical even small changes, contributions, or errors become. Accordingly, those at the top tend to interfere with the nominal heads of major projects.

As Churchill once quipped, "War is too important to be left to generals."

Nearly everyone makes the transition from trainee to Young Turk. Some "sink or swim" training programs even combine the two phases.

Once you've completed the Young Turk phase, you move on through a series of mid-level jobs until you reach a position of leadership we refer to as the "general manager." For our purposes, the "mid-level" breakpoints are similar even among the wide number of jobs that may be included at that level, and so we've made no attempt to differentiate between mid-level positions.

Once you reach the general manager level, however, the leadership responsibilities you'll have will generate their own special breakpoints. Accordingly, we've separated this level from the others for special discussion.

Similarly, an officer and chief executive each have special forces operating to influence their performance. Accordingly, we discuss each of these two top levels separately.

We then move on to describe special demands on the post-CEO stage we refer to as "advisory power," and, finally, to describe the major concerns that most executives face during retirement years.

THE TWO CAREER PATHS

A key additional factor we've learned over the years at G&S is that the demands on you at a given career level will vary depending on the level you're ultimately trying to attain. Put another way, your own ambitions for the future affect your performance needs for the present. If you set your career sights on a chief executive's spot, you'll have a different set of demands than if you're simply looking to stay at your present level or perhaps move up to a general manager's or officer's position. It's as if two paths diverge after the Young Turk phase. We call the path that leads to the CEO spot the "fast track" and the other route the "steady path."

We've diagrammed the two career paths below. Whether you choose (or appear to choose) one or the other can be all-important to your career progress.

manufactured products. In short order, he had turned the business around and was headed for success. Unfortunately, he underestimated the occurrence of tolerance error with higher volume, and when a huge government order was accepted, he was unable to deliver an acceptable product at a profit. He lost the company a great deal of money. The result was that his peer group, mostly executives four to five years older than he, smugly consoled themselves that this young upstart had finally been stopped.

His frustration, unfortunately, was just beginning. Having decided to leave the company, he found that his income and position at Bendix were now at a level where, when he interviewed outside, he was in competition with that same group of four- to five-year-older executives. The better companies in most cases would opt for the solid, seasoned ten-year veteran over the well-publicized young exec, which left him with the prospect of working for what he considered to be second- or third-rate companies. He fell into the classic trap: moving too quickly without building the necessary foundation and power base before a final assault.

Lee Iacocca had his power base in place prior to his move to Chrysler.

If you're on the fast track, you must choose your assignments carefully. A critical element of each new assignment should be the expansion of your talent base. With wider experience, you not only need more responsibility, you also need more *key* responsibility. For example, if sales is your specialty, it's not enough to be head of sales to keep you moving toward the top—you've got to be head of sales at a company where sales is *the* key function. If the company is sales-driven, you will deal with other division heads, but you will have more leadership clout when it comes to making real policy decisions to meet overall corporate objectives. In the process, you get more general leadership/management experience required for the next step up toward the chief executive's spot.

For managers aspiring to the top job, this particular "right church, wrong pew" problem has been one of the most common frustrations over the years, so address it early on. Ask yourself regularly: What drives this company? Am I a directly influencing factor in its growth, or am I moving off track? If you work for a direct-selling company like Avon, Mary Kay, or Electrolux, the answer will usually be clear. However most corporate cultures are less clear, and you'll need to be alert to changes at the top affecting your progress. Changes may occur over an extended period—as they did with the Gillette Company, which moved from an engineering orientation to marketing and sales. Or changes may come rapidly, as Chrysler changed with Lee Iacocca's arrival.

While timing and some luck are important, you must watch and evaluate trends. So doing, you'll either stay ahead of the pack or see the handwriting on the wall.

Sometimes the negative effects of such broad trends can be hard to spot —particularly if they're industry-wide.

I recall that in the early 1970s many of the nation's largest banks were in the process of reevaluating how products were marketed to the consumer. Citicorp, Chase, and others were convinced that the traditional consumer packaged goods approach to marketing was the answer. They launched a flurry of recruiting activity targeted to attract high-powered consumer-marketing talent. Executives from General Foods, Procter & Gamble, Colgate, Lever Brothers, and General Mills were wooed from the marketing Halls of Ivy to pursue the mission.

Things went well for a time, particularly in the credit card businesses, but as rapidly as the trend had begun, frustration set in. The basic problem was not with the transference of skills, as many had initially thought. Rather, the problem was that marketing executives withered on the vine. The banks were for the most part led and directed by officers raised in the world of banking. The route to the top had been through those channels considered to be the bank's *line* businesses. And that route didn't change. The business of the bank was still banking, not marketing.

While new marketing groups attracted the attention of the press, many of the transported executives, accustomed to functioning in the mainstream limelight of their former employers, now found they were considered staff advertising and promotion additions to assist the "real" line managers. Those executives in institutional banking, commercial lending, etc., still found their way to the top. The consumer marketers were left to be content that their efforts were perhaps helpful to the overall group goals.

What was true for Citicorp and Chase in the 1970s still applies today in many industries like high tech. If you want the top jobs, position yourself in the "bottom line" areas where the company makes its money.

Your Alternative: The Steady Path

But do you really want the top job? That's the question you should ask yourself, and consider your alternative career track: the one we call the steady path.

You should be aware of its benefits. Generally, you'll have less pressure, less stress, less instability, and you can still look forward to very respectable earning power. Also, while the odds are against you, you may still have a shot at the top job. As you master your work, if you want more responsibility, take the option of moving from the stage of mid-level manager up to the general manager or officer level, where you have departmental authority over your function.

As a manager or officer on the steady path you might be head of sales for a company where sales is not considered the major function. Unlike your counterparts on the fast track, you would not be expected to move up to succeed. On the steady path, you don't have to diversify, to deal with more general problems, and you're not under so much pressure. As one of our clients stated, "The torpedoes coming your way aren't going to sink the ship."

Yet the steady-path career levels offer real opportunities for growth and achievement. Because you've been around long enough to know the ropes, you'll be viewed as a "pro." Within your sphere of influence, you can become the recognized authority. As time goes on, you'll gain increased respect and autonomy of the chief executive and advisory power phases, yet without the pressure. People will come to you for leadership, though you're not being paid to take responsibility for what you recommend. You're a guru. They'll come to seek your opinions, though they won't have to act upon them. You can continue on the steady path right up until retirement.

Which career path is right for you? Should you go for the top spot and select the fast track, or should you look to the less stressful rewards of the steady path?

HOW TO USE THIS BOOK

Prior to selecting your career path, you should have a clear picture of where your career destination lies. In other words, you should know the kind of job you ultimately want, and the kind of job where you can realistically expect to do your best work. To help you arrive at your career goals and evaluate your present conditions and future opportunities, we include in Chapter 4 special tests we've developed for these purposes.

To help you decide between the fast track and the steady path, we've devoted Chapter 5 to a test that can give you a strong indication of where your real preferences lie.

Once you've taken the tests in Chapters 4 and 5, you'll have a clear idea where your career destination lies and what path to take to get there.

Then you can use the remaining chapters of BREAKPOINTS to help you recognize and deal with breakpoints you'll encounter during your career.

Some of these breakpoints apply to every career phase. We call these "universal" breakpoints and list the ten we consider most important in Chapter 6. You should thoroughly familiarize yourself with these key events and with recommendations on how to successfully maximize opportunities they present, for more likely than not you'll encounter each one as you progress.

In addition to universal breakpoints, however, you should know the special breakpoints associated with each of the career stages you're planning to enter. We've devoted a separate chapter to the major breakpoints that arise from your performance, from your personal life, and from your "political" work relationships at each career stage. Because the selection of fast track or steady path will make a difference in the demands on you at each career stage, we've made separate chapters for each stage at each career path.

Which of these chapters should you read? If you're already at the general manager level, it's doubtful whether your career plans will require you to read the trainee or Young Turk material—unless you decide to change fields and go back to square one again. We recommend that you begin with the career stage you're in now, and follow it with the career stage directly above you and the career stage that's your current goal. You should also read the material for your counterpart on the other career path; if you're a fast-track general manager, take a look at the breakpoints your steady-path colleague is encountering, and vice versa, because some of these breakpoints will also apply to you.

If you're thinking of starting out in business for yourself, and your test results indicate you're well suited for an entrepreneurial spot, you'll also want to read Chapter 15, our description of the breakpoints that confront the "instant chief executive."

If you're within ten years of retirement age, we also recommend that you read Chapter 18, "Retirement: The Story Continues." We make this recommendation because our experience has shown that long-range planning is a major component of retirement success.

Though not required reading, the chapters dealing with career phases other than those we've just mentioned may also be useful. They may help you to evaluate your own performance in earlier career stages, and to put any mistakes you may have made in proper perspective. Alternatively, these chapters on the early career phases may be of help to you if your job responsibilities include managing trainees, Young Turks, and mid-level managers. By understanding the breakpoint forces at work at their career levels, you may be able to counsel and manage them more effectively. You may also find that it pays to read the chapters that relate to your boss's career stage. By understanding the forces that affect your boss, you'll be better able to provide what your boss needs—and to understand why the management direction and motivation you're getting from your boss may be less than ideal.

To sum up, use the career-phase chapters for your own career planning by reading about the stage you're in now and the stages where you want to go. Use this book to improve your own performance as a manager by reading those chapters that apply to your subordinates. Use this book to improve your relations with your superiors by reading the chapters that apply to your boss's career stage.

We wish you well as you begin.

Chapter 4

Test Yourself
Part I: Creating Your Career Chart

How can you decide where you *really* want to be in your career?

Most people don't know the answer to this, because they haven't taken time to track where they've been or where they're going. Typically, people rationalize or second-guess. They say they're too busy with the demands of their jobs. Perhaps they concentrate on personal tasks such as taxes or paying the bills and meeting other responsibilities, relegating questions about what they really want to do with their lives to a far, far distant category of daydreams and idle speculation. Whether out of pride or fear, they often seem to shy away from thinking about what they'd *really* like to be doing, since that would mean, perhaps, identifying frustration, admitting that things haven't gone quite right and that they're not really happy. They say things like "No one's really happy," or "You work to get paid, period," and let it go at that.

You can also distract yourself from your real career goals by asking the *wrong* questions—trying to peer into the future and second-guess what your superiors are up to. The manager's all-time number-one nemesis is the crystal ball, because trying to peer into the future is all too tempting. If I'd been paid one dollar for all the crystal-ball conversations I've had with people over the years, the proceeds could buy me a small island in the Pacific complete with plantation and staff.

While we all need to evaluate our options, the options you see in the crystal ball aren't real. A real option for career advancement is a choice *you* can exercise. If you spend weeks, days, or even hours considering the impact of someone else's promotion, how old the managers above you are, how an individual's leaving the company may affect you, you're evaluating options you don't have power to exercise—and you're wasting time. More importantly, if you make career decisions based upon what you've seen in the crystal ball, you're navigating with your eyes shut.

A good example of how dangerous this can be came recently when I talked with a Xerox executive who was bemoaning his fate. Orange lights were flashing in the national economy. Xerox was under competitive pressure from foreign manufacturers, and making cutbacks. He assumed these omens cast a pall on his chances for promotion. To make a long story short, rather than discuss his future and career path with management, he chose to quietly pursue options outside the company. When he announced his resignation some months later, he was shocked to be told that he had indeed been considered on the fast track, and that a significant promotion had been just around the corner. His crystal ball let him down.

It's relatively easy to hide from the really important career questions for a while—or to obscure them with crystal-ball musings. Put on a firm smile and keep plugging. Admire yourself for being stoic. But if you're plugging, what are you plugging toward? Even if you "just work to get paid," to provide for yourself and your family, would you stop a moment and consider something that would make you a *better* provider?

We've seen thousands of clients who've been "rejuvenated" by the experience of getting their own career goals in order for the first time. We know how much it can help. In the long run, the experience pays off in productivity and earning power with returns far greater than the initial time or effort required. We've seen the effect on so many of the day-to-day problems, the fears and anxieties that lead to indecisiveness and hesitation on the job. When a client gets "on track" and knows where his career is going, these problems seem to fade away. A new kind of confidence develops, from a deep-down sense that what's being worked for is *really* right.

One morning I was having breakfast with an old friend and client of the firm we'll call Tom. He was running through his career background, which included Ralston Purina, Pillsbury, American Can, and Squibb. As we spoke, I discovered somewhat to my surprise that Tom was centering his career focus on general management issues broadly rather than his particular strength, which had always been new products.

When I asked him about this, he reacted with shock, saying that while his interests had always been creative, his real strength, he believed, was in running something large. After an hour or so of strong discussion, Tom conceded that while, yes, he was a good people manager, he was an outstanding new-product expert. After some further discussion, he joined the excellent Marketing Corporation of America, where he did an outstanding job for several years as a consultant. Today he's the head of his own small new-product consulting firm in New England—a long way from his former objective to run something large.

The tests you'll find here—and in Chapter 5—help you bring your career goals into focus. These tests apply the Goodrich & Sherwood career-analysis method—a proven technique that's worked for thousands of key executives. Once you've completed the career analysis, you'll be in a position to set your own sights. Then you can fully utilize the other chapters of BREAKPOINTS—making the appropriate moves to get where you *really* want to be. You should provide yourself with every opportunity available—otherwise you're cheating yourself, whether you're in high school or approaching retirement with a new life and perhaps a new career to manage.

Capsule Summary

The tests we recommend for your career chart self-analysis cover three major areas. The first is your Personal Satisfaction Index—we call it the PSI. The PSI measures your general level of satisfaction—based on factors *you* consider most important. You customize the index to your individual preferences. By retaking the PSI test every six months, you'll have a clear indication of whether your trend is up or down or whether you're in a position to profit from a career move.

The second major test is your asset inventory. We've developed this instrument to encourage you to record on paper your capabilities and strong points—your career assets. Be honest but brag a little. You'll use the asset inventory to prepare your résumé and to take stock of your career potential when evaluating your opportunities. As a manager, you can use this instrument to evaluate your subordinates when selecting them for new assignments. You can also use this tool when preparing job requirements for new employees. It is helpful in spotting talent complementary to yours and provides guidance for others doing the hiring.

You may also want to use your asset inventory as a companion piece to the standardized tests for personal preference and personal aptitude that are available through Goodrich & Sherwood and other counseling offices and through university testing centers. We don't include those entire tests here, of course, since the answers are proprietary and the results should be interpreted by someone with the training for an accurate evaluation.

The third area for your self-analysis is a collection of separate tests designed to make you "breakpoint-sensitive." You can use these tests from time to time—particularly when your PSI has dropped or risen by ten points. The breakpoint sensitizers should be read in conjunction with the "Top 10" chapter of this book and with the career phase chapters that apply to the career phase you're in now, to the career phase you're about to enter, and to your ultimate career target phase.

When you've completed this testing chapter, you're ready to fill in your career path.

YOUR PERSONAL SATISFACTION INDEX

How are you doing? You know the thousand and one responses you give automatically to this greeting every day. "About half." "Not too bad." "Okay, thanks." "Pretty good." "Can't complain." "Fair enough." And so forth. These automatic responses of course don't convey much information. They're not meant to. In fact, people probably aren't too interested. But prior to making any career decisions, you *should* know how you're doing. Remember the rule of navigation: Before proceeding, determine where you are. That's why we developed the Personal Satisfaction Index.

"Wait a minute," we can hear you saying. "Why do I need a test to tell me whether I'm satisfied or not? I know darn well if I'm happy. I know when I'm not happy. I can feel it. There's no point wasting time with a test."

We don't agree. Because human beings are infinitely adaptable, over a period of time we can adapt to intolerable conditions—rationalizing what we wouldn't have put up with on a bet in previous years. And because we human beings tend toward black-and-white decisions, our feelings about life circumstances can be colored by day-to-day events—or by problems that are temporary.

We need, in short, an objective measure—like the PSI—which monitors trends rather than emotional highs and lows. And though the PSI will not render you completely objective about your career while you're suffering from a recent lecture from the boss, we have found that by quantifying and analyzing your career components logically, you will make better decisions than by reacting through a seat-of-the-pants feeling that "things are/are not okay."

YOUR CAREER COMPONENTS

How, then, do you quantify how you're doing?

To begin, decide what's important to you—what you want out of your career life. You can also use this index to evaluate non-career components —your relationship with your family, for example, or your intellectual pursuits or hobbies. But for career purposes, we recommend that you leave out specific points of non-career components so you don't muddy the waters.

Don't create categories that show how your putting game is progressing, or whether you need to work on your forehand smash or backhand lob strokes. Instead include, if important, the way your career has an impact on hobbies like golf and tennis. For example, "I have as much time as I need to play golf." "My geographic location lets me enjoy skiing as often as I'd like."

Similarly, include among your components the ways your career impacts on your personal relationships, rather than the way you're managing the relationships themselves. For example, "My job gives me enough time to spend with my family." "My work location is close enough to the good schools my family needs." Leave out components of your life such as "I'm doing well at providing disciplined leadership for my children"—unless you can see a direct link between your career and this component. For example, "I'm so tense after a day at work that I'm not doing a good job raising my children."

We include a sample column of components on the next page. You'll see how they're arranged in groups such as geographic area, industry, company, position, and people you encounter on the job. You'll also see that our sample candidate decided that some of the categories weren't important enough to apply to this case, and so marked them "N/A." Feel free to add or delete. We keep the group categories for convenience so you can spot the patterns of satisfaction—or lack thereof.

PERSONAL SATISFACTION INDEX

1	2	3	4	5	6
Career Component Name	Priority Rating	Current Rating	Weighted Rating (#2 × #3)	Index Base (Add #4; divide by sum of #2)	Index Score (#5 × 10)
GEOGRAPHIC AREA					
climate good	1	10	10		
has good schools	5	10	50		
progressive community	N/A	N/A	N/A		
entertainment	1	5	5		
shopping	2	10	20		
sports/recreation	3	10	30		
convenient for travel	N/A	N/A	N/A		
other companies in my industry located here	4	10	40		
	16		155	9.69	97
INDUSTRY					
growth area	3	7	21		
respected field	3	6	18		
recession-proof	3	5	15		
	9		54	6.0	60
COMPANY					
high market share	4	5	20		
culture fits my style	4	7	28		
respected in industry	4	7	28		
promotes from within	5	10	50		
	17		126	7.41	74
POSITION					
pay	5	6	30		
my skills are growing	5	9	45		
learning curve still trends up	N/A	N/A	N/A		
what I do is satisfying	5	9	45		
prestige is adequate	4	8	32		
my performance is important to company	5	9	45		
	24		197	8.21	82
PEOPLE					
boss is helpful	3	6	18		
boss is competent	5	6	30		
boss can help me move up	5	9	45		

1	2	3	4	5	6
Career Component Name	Priority Rating	Current Rating	Weighted Rating (#2 × #3)	Index Base (Add #4; divide by sum of #2)	Index Score (#5 × 10)
associates are competent	4	7	28		
associates are supportive	2	10	20		
associates are people I like	3	9	27		
	22		168	7.64	76
TOTAL	88		646	7.34	73

COMPONENT PRIORITY

You'll list the components in a column in whatever order they come to mind. But, obviously, some are or will be more important than others. To differentiate among them, we rank each component on a scale of 1 through 5. You can assign numbers to each on an abstract basis if you feel most comfortable with this method, but we recommend you write out value descriptions next to each on a list such as the one we include here and rate from 1 to 5.

I want this now. (multiply by 5—top priority)
I'd like to have this in the next twelve months. (multiply by 4—second priority)
This is a two-year goal. (multiply by 3—third priority)
I want this within five years. (multiply by 2—fourth priority)
This would be nice someday. (multiply by 1—least priority)

Having the value descriptions handy to refer to as you're ranking helps you to remain objective regarding the components or groups of components. Refer to the words you used to describe numerical values as you rank all the components in priority.

THE COMPONENT INDEX

The third step in your Personal Satisfaction Index is to rate the way you feel about each of the career components at this point in your life. For a rating, use a 5 through 10 scale, with 10 being the top rank and 5 being below "passing." Again, we recommend you use some value description next to each number to keep your replies consistent. You can use the descriptions we provide below, or whatever you want to substitute.

Excellent, meeting all my objectives. (10)
Not a problem. (9)
Okay, status quo. (8)
Sometimes dissatisfied about this. (7)
Frequently dissatisfied about this. (6)
Constantly dissatisfied about this. (5)

YOUR OVERALL INDEX

To get your overall rating, multiply your component rating by its priority rating and enter the result in column 4. Then add column 2 and divide the result into the sum of the components in column 4. Then multiply the result by 10. If you gave each component a rating of 10, you'd have a score of 100. As you're making your ratings, bear in mind all the maxims you've learned about life this side of Nirvana and about nothing being perfect.

Your overall index gives you the general drift of how you're doing. If you fill out your PSI chart with its components and continue to take the same test every six months or so, at regular intervals, you'll have a good baseline from which to judge whether you're making career progress—or whether your new job that was billed as a "career advancement" is really having a less than beneficial effect on your personal satisfaction. If you're unhappy, you may wish to shorten the cycle to every two or three months to monitor trends more closely.

As an additional tool for planning career moves, you can develop a subindex rating for each of the major component groups. Simply add the priority ratings you've placed in column 2 for each component subgroup, divide them into the total of column 4 for each subgroup, and then multiply by 10. The example we've given shows the geography subgroup rating as the best score, with industry, company, and people subgroups giving the least satisfaction.

For this person, the chart indicates that a change of jobs to the same type of position in another company would be desirable—provided that a long-distance move is not involved.

We recommend that before making a career move that would affect any one of these components, you first take a look at your rating. If there's not much room for improvement, think twice before making any change. Remember, in spite of a relatively low score, you know what you have at present. A new career is filled with unknowns, both positive and negative.

I recall an executive with Richardson-Vicks who filled out his PSI for five years and finally got to a rating of 96. He came to us after he'd received a job offer to move across the country with a newly formed high-tech company—one of the "ground floor" deals that promise tremendous reward but also carry substantial risk. We looked at his PSI of 96 and asked if he was telling the truth when he filled out the index.

He allowed he was. "I really do feel good about what I'm doing."

There was a long silence. He looked at his PSI and then at me with a sheepish grin. "I see what you mean," he said. "Whatever this job has, it can't get much better than what I've got now. And it sure could get a heck of a lot worse."

He didn't take the job. The postscript to the story is that the newly formed company went belly-up eighteen months later. As it turned out, the executive was promoted and has been updating his PSIs ever since.

We hope that you find this a valuable monitoring and planning instrument. Remember, like any tool, it's effective in your hands only to the degree that you apply skill and judgment. It contains *your* values exclusively, and must be updated from time to time in both the components column and the priorities column, as your values, objectives, and priorities change over the years.

YOUR ASSET INVENTORY

"I went to a career counselor," one southwestern newspaper publisher likes to say, "and took the full battery of tests. The result was that the counselor told me I had two choices. Either I could start a small-town newspaper in Lubbock, Texas, or I could raise begonias in Illinois. I'm allergic to flowers, so here I am as publisher of the *Globe.*"

This story reflects the mystique that often is attached to career "placement" tests. Rarely can a test give you the precise direction toward two specific jobs, much less two specific job locations. People—regrettably some career counselors among them—may *claim* scientific precision for recommendations that they base on test batteries, but no reputable career counselor can provide a mandate for a choice of only two jobs. People are too adaptable, and test instruments too imprecise.

If you came to Goodrich & Sherwood for testing, we'd give you a battery of personal preference, personality, and aptitude tests all the same. We have found that they're invaluable in uncovering areas perhaps missed or in pinpointing need for change where the traits of an individual don't seem to mesh with what the job calls for.

We don't include these tests here, of course, since they're proprietary, and also since the results should be interpreted by a professional with background to relate one set of test results to another and determine how the overall pattern set forth in the results applies to a given set of job opportunities.

For your self-evaluation, however, we highly recommend the asset inventory instrument. As with the components of PSI, the components here are generated by you alone, so you can better identify your own unique strengths.

The test is based on the "critical incident technique" developed by Dr. J. C. Flanagan, a psychologist for the U.S. Air Force, during the beginning years of World War II, when there was a shortage of pilots. In order to determine component skills involved in the job of pilot so that proper training could be performed, Dr. Flanagan needed to learn what made a good pilot. At first attempt, the people he interviewed were well intentioned but not very helpful. Dr. Flanagan came away learning only that a good pilot had to be stable, conscientious, have good vision, good reflexes, be loyal, and so on. Not much to build a crash training program around.

To identify specific skills, Dr. Flanagan developed the critical incident technique. Establishing a model, he asked expert pilots, "Tell me an instance where a pilot performed really well." Then he analyzed what the pilot did in that situation—what skills and traits resulted in the behavior the pilot exhibited.

We utilize a similar technique here. You ask yourself, "When was I performing really well?" Write down five "incidents" during your life when you were performing *really* well. We supply two here as examples only.

Incident	Skill	Personality Trait
1 Negotiated rent increase with angry tenant	Anticipating "opponents'" needs; financial projections	Patience; sincerity
2 Prepared complex lease on short notice	Writing; knowledge of landlord-tenant law	Work under pressure; patience

Now write down five instances when you were really enjoying yourself at work. Again, we supply two examples.

1 Prepared newsletter for investors	Writing; financial analysis	Creativity; selling talent
2 Made speech to local realtors' board	Speaking; organization	Creativity; "ham"

Now, as we have done here, break out in a second column the *major* skill that you drew on to perform well, or that you enjoyed the most. In the third column, write down the most important personality trait enabling you to "win" in this particular critical incident. Beneath each skill, write the *next* most important skill.

After you've completed this analysis for each of the ten critical incidents you've listed, you should have twenty skills and twenty personality traits. What are the skills and personality traits that occur most frequently? These are your assets, and these are what you do best.

Identifying these skills can make an enormous difference in your career objectives. For example, a number of years ago an old friend and client I'll call Jerry and I were having lunch. Jerry was at that time a senior executive at Johnson & Johnson in charge of mergers and acquisitions. He was recounting with great excitement some of his experiences in this area. Jerry was well suited for his job because he had an unusual career track, starting out with a pharmacy major in college and progressing to new products and marketing at J&J. As the conversation continued, it became clear to both of us that Jerry's technical expertise, coupled with creativity and negotiating skill, could open new fields for him.

He approached Morton Davis, one of the most successful venture capitalists in the United States to seek his advice. Davis hired Jerry on the spot and put him into a key position in his company, D. H. Blair. Jerry went into action immediately. He decided to concentrate on the health-care industry field he knew well and within six months had Wall Street buzzing. In his first year, he had broken all records at D. H. Blair and was on his way to a new career. Today, Jerry is president of a rapidly growing investment capital and brokerage firm specializing in the health-care industry. He is a leader in the industry and has a wonderful future ahead of him.

When you've identified your career assets, we recommend that you combine them with the values and preferences you've identified in your Personal Satisfaction Index to create a "Personal Profile." Your Personal Profile summarizes on a single page what you want from your work and what assets you bring to your job. It's for your own use, so be completely candid—don't think of it as a résumé. The act of creating the profile and revising it from time to time is what gives this instrument its value. The exercise helps you become a more expert "shopper" in the job marketplace, because you'll evaluate what you're looking for and where you can best fit in. More important, creating your Personal Profile will increase your chances of getting that ideal job, because you'll be fully prepared for those two most common interview questions: "Why should we hire you?" and "What makes you think you'd like to work here?"

SAMPLE PROFILE

Marcia first started her career by obtaining her pharmacy degree and then working at several pharmacies over a period of four years. She then decided to move into business, working as a manager in the research and development division of a drug company. Marcia is a very energetic, active person who began to feel bored after three years at the company. Here's how Marcia completed her profile.

CATEGORY	CHARACTERISTICS	
CAREER ASSETS SKILLS	Has degree in pharmacy, Pharmacy experience, Laboratory experience, Managed staff of six.	Technical training and experience in pharmacy and new drugs development. Some management ability.

CATEGORY	CHARACTERISTICS	
PERSONAL STYLE/ MOTIVATION	Enjoys the outdoors, active, enjoys fast pace. Good with a wide variety of people. Motivated to earn high salary. Bored easily with status quo.	Outgoing, people-oriented. Needs change. Marks success through money.
WORK ENVIRONMENT PREFERRED	Size of company not important. Likes environment where people work autonomously. Prefers to stay in company selling drugs and/or medical supplies.	Enjoys kind of company that matches her background.

As Marcia reviewed her background, she came to realize that she wasn't happy in her present job function, which appeared too administrative and technical rather than people-oriented. Combining this preference with her outgoing personality and drive to earn money, Marcia saw that she was ideally suited to sales. Thus her next career move was to ask to be transferred over to the sales division where she could better apply her talents and interests.

BREAKPOINT SENSITIVITY TESTS

It's often astonishing to me how people can block out reality. As anyone who's observed a parlor hypnotist has seen, we're all capable of ignoring pinpricks of real pain or of believing that an ice cube is red-hot to the touch. Regrettably, we can be just as inaccurate in our perceptions about "realities" in our jobs. Blocking out can be done with the best of motives, and in some cases is a better course than, for instance, losir з control, but it's nonetheless dangerous. To ignore signals that indicate you're in career trouble isn't "positive thinking." This avoidance is dangerous to your career.

We've developed breakpoint sensitivity tests to jog your alertness and awareness. You should skim this section from time to time, preferably when you're in a neutral frame of mind. Some of the results may leap out at you one year and not another, depending upon your circumstances and mental attitude at the time.

To further increase awareness, read the chapters in this book that apply to your current career phase, the career phase you're about to enter, and the career phase representing your ultimate goal.

I. "Look Inward" Tests

These are essential. Without them, you're steering your ship without direction or destination. Okay perhaps for a Sunday afternoon sail, but not to plot a lifetime cruise.

Test Your Goals. Plot your goals and identify where you want to be five years from now. Consider achievement, location, status, activity skills, money, whatever's important. Define the position you want to be in.

Now, where do you want to be ten years from now?

Where are your five- and ten-year points on our career diagram?

Keep in mind that your target positions may be outside the current job environment. You may want to use your job primarily as a steady source of income, while developing real career challenge in anything from political office to writing novels or raising a family.

One of our clients, the publisher of a major U.S. men's magazine, told me that his real objective in building a strong management team was to provide the base and freedom for him to pursue his real interest in the field of politics long-term.

We applied this strategy several years ago, when an executive with General Foods Corporation came to my office. During the course of our discussion about his career, he remarked about a fine framed collection of antique English salmon-fishing flies on my wall and told me of his hobby making and selling fishing lures. In short order the conversation had shifted from food to fishing, and we had hit upon his career choice. He continued for a time at GF, but today is, I believe, president of his own fishing lure company, his real career.

When you've identified your target positions, make a list of the steps you'll need to get there. Look at those who've already reached your target position. What was their background? Where did they come from? What career "ladder" did they use? Are you on the ladder? Should you be? If you are, where are you on that ladder? What's your logical next step up?

What skills do you need to make that next step? If you can't get what you need from where you are, you've got to move either inside the company or outside.

Test Your Performance. Is your current job challenging? If you've "got it in your hip pocket," ask yourself if your target position, your real career challenge, is outside the workplace. If it is, fine, provided your company doesn't subscribe to the "up or out" philosophy. If it does, however, or if your real career goal lies elsewhere within the workplace, you should start planning a near-term job change.

An interesting new trend is evolving that should be noted here. Several companies, the most notable perhaps being IBM Corporation, have set up or sponsored employees leaving to pursue entrepreneurial career paths in areas that are of interest to the company long-term. Recognizing that they were about to lose a talented person and perhaps a shot at a major technological advance, these companies have been able to get the best of both worlds, as, in many cases, has the employee.

Test Your Behavior. Are you overcompensating for missed career satisfaction? There are many indicators, from starting one hobby after another to excessive drinking, gambling, or frequent love affairs. Don't confuse working toward a target position outside the workplace with this type of overcompensation. This behavior, often described as a mid-life crisis, is non-productive, time-killing activity, not positive, goal-seeking activity. Many are the executives who burned out midway through a promising career by losing control and direction.

The "Symptoms" Test. In fact, your physician may be able to tell that you're unhappy from symptoms of stress or depression or physical breakdowns such as ulcers. So, incidentally, may your spouse or close family members.

The "Wake-up" Test. If you're planning your workday when you wake up, you're more likely satisfied than if your workday is the furthest thing from your mind. This is not to say that you must be consumed and excited about your job every morning. However, if negative feelings persist morning after morning, something is wrong.

II. "Look Upward" Tests

The "Watch the Boss" Test. If your boss is considered successful, and you can do well 80 percent of what your boss does, you're probably ready to move up.

But be careful. Do you want to be where your boss is?

Ask the Boss. Use the direct approach. Some people are afraid of negative feedback, but you can quickly find out where you stand at minimal risk if you know the right approach. You'll then have an idea of not only where you stand but what you have to do to get on track. Perhaps it would be easier to pursue your career elsewhere. The key is to emphasize that you want to perform well for the company—avoid any hint of an ultimatum. Asking, "What do you think I should focus on for the next five years?" will get you a better response than "I'm thinking about my career options—where do I stand here?"

III. "Look Outward" Tests

The "Results" Test. Are you producing as well as or better than those at your level? Measure the results you generated in terms of profit to the company. What do you bring to the bottom line? Then compare the amount of time and effort expended to achieve the results. If you're putting in less effort and producing as much as or more than those at your level, you're probably ready to move up. If you're putting in more time and producing less or just staying even, that's a danger signal.

The "Value" Test. How does your pay compare with that of the others at your level? It's difficult to uncover this information, but it can be invaluable. Your boss correlates pay with results, value, attitude, and commitment. Who's perceived as giving the company the best results for the money? If it's you, you're ready to move up. If you're being paid more than those at your level and are not slated for promotion, you're in a danger zone. Unless you're achieving more, you're on your way out. If you're being paid less, you're a bargain—or perhaps are of less value.

The "Company Culture" Test. Is your management made up of proponents of physical fitness? Are you an overweight smoker? If so, even if your days aren't numbered at the company, your opportunity level certainly is limited. Mismatches with other facets of your corporate culture may also limit your potential.

I recall clearly a plaintive phone call from a senior manager at a Texas-based airline several years ago who felt his career was at a standstill because several of the senior executives liked to carouse and carry on until the wee hours of the morning. The caller was happily married and had no intention of partaking. Over time, he complained, he found himself excluded from the "in" group. This person left the airline and is now the head of a sizable company where he has established a very different culture. The airline, interestingly enough, is defunct.

While there are exceptions, most corporate leaders prefer their employees to be led by someone they recognize as "one of us."

The "Leverage" Test. At company X, you need ten years' experience as regional manager before you move up. At company Y, you need only six. If you're at company X, you've got "leverage" to move over to Y as early as your fourth year (they'll want at least a year to get acquainted before they promote you). Variations in other criteria can also give leverage. The number of accounts you handled, or your annual sales, or the number of people you're supervising may be enough to get you promoted right now —somewhere else. So take a close look at the competition. Perhaps you'll receive a healthy salary increase in the process. It could save you a lot of time by shortening a cycle and starting you at a higher salary in a new salary-scaled position.

YOUR CAREER CHART

Now that you have an idea of the kind of position your assets fit, and you've thought about what's important to you for your longer-term personal satisfaction, you're ready to prepare your career chart. We've included a blank form drawn along the lines of the sample career chart, but with more levels to indicate the varying jobs you'll hold at mid-level manager, general manager, and so on while moving toward your career objective.

Chapter 5

Test Yourself

Part II: Fast Track, Steady Path, or Entrepreneur?

Capsule Summary

When should you test your career-path motives?

When you reach mid-level management, it's time to confirm that you're on the right career path. During the earlier career stages, your primary goal has been to adapt to the world of work and to establish yourself as a force your superiors can count on. Caught up in the day-to-day melee, you may be more concerned with survival than with your ultimate career goal, which may be decades away.

But when you've passed through the Young Turk stage, when you're committing funds for your company or representing the company on the outside, it's time to look again at where you want to go.

Why a second look? There are a number of reasons.

First, the stakes are high. The fast track has many frustrations, commitments, and demands. Before subjecting yourself to more of the same for years to come, you should know where you really want to be.

Second, you may not know your options. You may think that you need to stay on the fast track to survive. That's probably incorrect. In most companies you needn't do all the "right" things required to reach the corner office in order to keep your job.

Third, your drive to reach the top may not be genuine. We're all conditioned by daily bombardment of media worship of "leadership," "vision," and "power." You may be subject to harangues about "survival of the fittest" from your boss. The result can create a drive to "reach the top" even when "the top" isn't where you want to be.

You may also be pressured into giving up your ambitions and getting off the fast track and into a business of your own. Media bombard us with "entrepreneurial" idols. With a current rate of 600,000 new businesses launched annually, today's advertisers are quick to romanticize the small-business market to sell products ranging from personal computers to beer, and just about everything in between. You need more than a yen to be your own boss, as witness the 200,000 companies who had to close their doors last year.

In short, it's easy to be bamboozled into getting off the fast track, and it's easy to be pressured into staying on. Making the wrong choice can be both personally and economically painful. Once you get off the fast track, it's difficult to return, particularly if you've been off for a time. We offer these caveats—and this test—to help you make sure you look before you leap. The questions below provide some tools to make an intelligent choice.

We recommend that you photocopy the answer sheet rather than mark in this book, so that you can take the test again and again. You should take the test at least once every year, for many reasons: Your personal values change with experience; your skills change with experience; the market for your skills changes as technology changes; and your industry changes from time to time.

You should also take this test anytime your PSI is at 90 or below in non-geographical items and you can't identify one overriding cause that is dragging down the index.

Here are the questions.

Check the column that applies.

	Agree	Disagree	Applies, But No Opinion	Doesn't Apply
1. I still consider myself a quick study.	____	____	____	____
2. I like to read the editorial page and the international pages				

of the newspaper, but I also enjoy the sports and business pages. ___ ___ ___ ___

3. I really want to be proud to be a part of the company I work for. ___ ___ ___ ___

4. I want to be part of a company that is the leader in its field. ___ ___ ___ ___

5. I like the way my wardrobe "fits the mold" at the company I work for. ___ ___ ___ ___

6. I've carefully chosen my clothes to reflect my own tastes. ___ ___ ___ ___

7. I want my car (my house, my apartment) to "say it all" about my ambitions and what kind of a person I am. ___ ___ ___ ___

8. I'm a self-starter and don't want outside motivation. ___ ___ ___ ___

9. I've succeeded in setting up a good mentor relationship with my boss. ___ ___ ___ ___

10. I want all the good advice that my "mentor" at work has to offer. ___ ___ ___ ___

11. I could get along very well without my boss's advice, even though he/she is right most of the time. ___ ___ ___ ___

12. It galls me that a few decisions I made last year cost the company more than they paid me. ___ ___ ___ ___

13. It galls me that I made so much more money for the company last year than I did for myself. ___ ___ ___ ___

14. I won't feel good and professional until I understand my job more thoroughly. ___ ___ ___ ___

	Agree	Disagree	Applies, But No Opinion	Doesn't Apply
15. I still don't have all the answers about my job, but I'm having a good time learning.	___	___	___	___
16. I wouldn't want to uproot my family for a risky business move.	___	___	___	___
17. I think of myself as a professional, but I don't want to be bound to a "specialty."	___	___	___	___
18. I'm putting too much of my energy into work to have any "side deals" going.	___	___	___	___
19. I'll always want a way to earn some money "on the side."	___	___	___	___
20. I've always been able to make time for social clubs and church groups.	___	___	___	___
21. I get a real charge out of speaking before a group.	___	___	___	___
22. It's amazing how many new theories are available to increase business productivity today.	___	___	___	___
23. Our company has leadership potential for the present marketplace and I want to be a key part of that effort to expand.	___	___	___	___
24. Our company's role in today's marketplace is just the way I'd like to see it continue.	___	___	___	___
25. Our company is missing the boat in today's market, and it's a real thorn in my side.	___	___	___	___

26. Someday I could see my-

self ready to "bet the ranch" on a big payoff opportunity.

27. Our company hires consultants and gets valuable perspective from the outside.

28. I really haven't bothered reading the consultants' reports, since they don't affect my job right now.

29. I wouldn't expect most consultants to know any more about my work than I do.

30. I'd never put my own money on a consultant's recommendation of something I didn't already agree on, so why hire one?

31. Our company's public image is much too sterile.

32. Our company's public image seems about right.

33. It galls me that our company's public image doesn't measure up to the image of its competitors.

34. From what I know of the competition, I could just as easily work there.

35. I always like a complete break from my work atmosphere at least two or three times per week.

36. I usually find ways to improve my performance during my leisure time.

37. I like to pick up work contacts by socializing.

38. I don't much plan ahead for my leisure activity.

	Agree	Disagree	Applies, But No Opinion	Doesn't Apply
39. I wouldn't let work interfere with a holiday.	___	___	___	___
40. I always push my subordinates when we've got to meet a deadline.	___	___	___	___
41. I'd let a deadline lapse to give a subordinate a chance to learn a new area.	___	___	___	___
42. I get a big charge out of seeing people under me learn new skills.	___	___	___	___
43. I'm a "Mr. Clean" kind of dresser and take pride in that image.	___	___	___	___
44. I'm my own boss in a lot of ways, even though I report up the ladder just like everyone else.	___	___	___	___
45. Someday I don't want to have to take any more of a boss's power-hungry ploys.	___	___	___	___
46. You've got to go along to get along in this world.	___	___	___	___
47. You really work for your family when all's said and done.	___	___	___	___
48. If you provide your family with high-quality experiences you make up for your absence at times.	___	___	___	___
49. My family needs a consistent, constant presence that I really want to provide.	___	___	___	___
50. I like getting out in the community and seeing who the power brokers are.	___	___	___	___

51. I like to read the local paper's local business section and see what all my friends are doing. ____ ____ ____ ____

52. Someday I'd like to coach Little League or kids' soccer or maybe be a Scout leader. ____ ____ ____ ____

53. Rather than coach a kids' team, I'd prefer to take my kids fishing or to a nature preserve or a historical landmark. ____ ____ ____ ____

54. It's amazing the kind of valuable tips you can find in magazines like the *Harvard Business Review* or the *Times* business section. ____ ____ ____ ____

55. I like *The Wall Street Journal* because it condenses the business news and splits it up so that I can skip what I don't want to bother with. ____ ____ ____ ____

56. I read the New York *Times* or *U.S. News* because I think that having an international perspective is important. ____ ____ ____ ____

57. I would seriously consider taking an M.B.A.-type seminar for a week abroad because I think it would give me a chance to profit from the perspectives of different nations and cultures. ____ ____ ____ ____

58. Financial planning isn't my cup of tea, and I have no interest in reading annual reports. ____ ____ ____ ____

59. I'd let my secretary pick the magazines for our department's reception area, but I'd check up on her from time to time. ____ ____ ____ ____

60. I think public relations is

	Agree	Disagree	Applies, But No Opinion	Doesn't Apply
important, but I'd prefer to hold up my own end of operations, and leave the PR to specialists.	___	___	___	___
61. When I introduce myself, I usually say my job title because I'm proud of it.	___	___	___	___
62. It's the bottom line that counts. I don't so much care how the job gets done as long as it's done.	___	___	___	___
63. I like to form a good, detailed plan of action and stick to it. If the results aren't what I hoped for, I'll go back to the drawing board.	___	___	___	___

Answers

In answering, be liberal in choosing the "Doesn't apply" category if part of the statement does not fit the situation. For example, if you've never considered yourself a quick study, answer "Doesn't apply" to the statement "I still consider myself a quick study."

If for some reason the explanation given in the answers below and your own reasons for making the choice are poles apart, feel free to disregard that question. (F = *fast track;* S = *steady path;* E = *entrepreneur)*

1. If you agree, score F. An ability to assimilate information quickly is one of the prerequisites of general management. If you disagreed or chose another column, score nothing.
2. If you agree, score F. A wide range of interests is helpful on the fast track, particularly economics and governmental policy.
3. If you agree, score F. An ability to identify with a company is essential to a fast-track attitude.
4. If you disagree, score E. The entrepreneur isn't so interested in being part of the company. He wants to *be* the company.

5. If you agree, score F. The ability to enjoy fitting the company mold is essential to be on the fast track.

6. If you agree, score E. Entrepreneurial types are more apt to be responsive to their own tastes rather than the company's.

7. If you disagree, score F. Fast-track mentality dictates that the style of your car or other public displays fit the company needs rather than your personal taste.

8. Score E if you agree. An entrepreneur is his own boss and resists outside motivation.

9. Score F if you agree. This may seem surprising, but the fast-track executive is very willing to learn from those above him.

10. Score E if you disagree. The entrepreneur is less likely to want the mentor relationship.

11. If you agree, score E, for the same reason as 10. The entrepreneur would rather go his own way, even at the cost of not being right.

12. If you agree, score S. The fast-track mentality is able to shrug off mistakes as the inevitable tuition for learning the next job up.

13. If you agree, score E. The entrepreneur is motivated toward number one.

14. If you agree, score S. The fast-track and entrepreneurial traits involve "faking it" as new responsibilities come faster than learning is possible.

15. If you agree, score F, for the same reason as 14.

16. If you disagree, score F. The ability to subordinate the ties your family has made with a community is essential to fast-track job changes.

17. If you agree, score F. The fast-track individual wants to generalize and have responsibility over a wide range of specialties.

18. If you agree, score F. Company loyalty and focus of energy on the job are essential parts of the fast-track motivation.

19. If you agree, score E. The entrepreneur is always looking for his own independent operations.

20. If you agree, score S. The fast-track and entrepreneurial minds will readily subordinate social activities to work.

21. If you agree, score F. The ability to enjoy public speaking is a big advantage to a fast-track career.

22. If you have no opinion, score S; if you agree, score F. The fast-track mentality is interested in business theories beyond the scope of his job, while the steady-path person is less likely to look that far.

23. If you disagree, score S. The steady-path person does not need the pressure of being a key part in the company's expansion.
24. If you have no opinion, score S. On the steady path you are less concerned with "big picture" items than with your own job.
25. If you agree, score F. The ability to be passionately concerned about a major policy issue is essential fast-track makeup.
26. If you agree, score E. The entrepreneur is ready to take this kind of risk.
27. If you agree, score F. The fast-track mentality wants outside data.
28. If you agree, score S. The steady path would prefer not to be distracted by material irrelevant to his or her own work.
29. If you agree, score E. The entrepreneur is unwilling to admit that his own knowledge is not sufficient.
30. If you agree, score E, for the same reason.
31. If you have no opinion, score S, since the steady-path mentality will not be bothered by these issues extraneous to the job.
32. If you agree, score S, for the same reason as 31.
33. If you agree, score F. The fast-track personality makeup will take major company policy issues to heart.
34. If you agree, score F. Even though loyalty is a part of the fast-track makeup, so is the ability to change companies.
35. If you agree, score S. The fast-track personality or entrepreneur will not be concerned about leisure.
36. If you agree, score F. The ability to mix business with pleasure is a fast-track trait.
37. If you disagree, score S. By keeping your work and social life separate, you're limiting your job's claim on your time.
38. If you agree, score E. The entrepreneur will typically not make plans for leisure, since his life is wrapped up in his business.
39. If you agree, score S. Subordinating work to outside priorities is a steady-path trait.
40. If you agree, score S. The steady-path criterion is getting the job done.
41. If you agree, score F. The fast-track manager is concerned with developing subordinates.
42. If you agree, score F, for the same reason as 41.
43. If you agree, score F. Taking pride in the traditional leadership image for business is a valuable fast-track trait.
44. If you agree, score S. The ability to see independence within the

chain of command is a steady-path characteristic, and suggests that the job's claim on you is limited.

45. If you agree, score E. The entrepreneur does not want any boss other than himself. Fast-track and steady-path people don't like power ploys either, but are willing to accept temporary subordination for the long-term goal.

46. If you disagree, score E. The entrepreneur is ready and willing to ruffle some feathers.

47. If you agree, score S. The claim of the job for the steady-path person is subordinated to family claims.

48. If you agree, score F. The fast-track mentality looks to the added opportunities the family gets from its enhanced position, rather than giving the family's claim for time priority over the job.

49. If you agree, score S. The steady-path person feels the opposite of the fast-track person on this issue.

50. If you agree, score F. The ability to identify community leaders and work with them is essential to top-level executive activity.

51. If you agree, score E. The fact that all your friends are local businessmen suggests that you will have a kindred entrepreneurial spirit.

52. If you agree, score F. The desire to bring group leadership into leisure time is a fast-track characteristic.

53. If you agree, score S. The choice of fishing or a more private activity suggests that the on-the-job exercise of leadership is one you'd rather leave behind in the workplace.

54. If you disagree, score E. The fast-track person will probably agree, and many steady-path counterparts will also, but the entrepreneur would rather go his own way.

55. If you agree, score F. The ability to skim effectively is an essential fast-track characteristic. So is the desire to absorb new information and eliminate the irrelevant.

56. If you agree, score F. The fast-track mentality wants to take the big-picture view.

57. If you agree, score F. The fast-track individual wants to broaden his or her perspective.

58. If you agree, score S. The steady-path makeup doesn't want to be bothered with irrelevant matters, but the concerns with financial planning or annual reports are the breath of life for the fast-track boardroom mentality and for many an entrepreneurial investor.

59. If you disagree, score F. Your concern for public image is commendable and probably not delegable (unless your secretary has unusual businesslike savvy regarding the tastes of your clients or those who frequent your reception room).

60. If you agree, score S, since you want to stay out of matters unconnected to your own job.

61. If you disagree, score E. The entrepreneur doesn't connect job title with self-worth. He or she connects *ownership* with self-worth.

62. If you agree, score E. Your fine disregard for procedure makes you subject to criticism by the organizational hierarchy above you—so you would prefer to dispense with that hierarchy.

63. If you agree, score S. Your desire to stick to a plan on the job without concern for the results until the end suggests that you want to limit your perspective and avoid the overall responsibility.

Remember to disregard answers if the reasoning doesn't apply.

You can now add the number of questions that indicated a preference for one of the three categories. You had

26 opportunities to score fast track;
21 to score steady path; and
17 to score entrepreneur.

You can get a sense of which path is best for you from the percentage of your scores in each category, based upon the opportunity to score in that category. If you scored 25 of the 26 fast-track questions with F, the odds favor your staying on the fast track. Determine your percentage for each category and compare them. If your scores are equally high for each career path, this indicates that your career thinking is in a state of confusion. Generally, if you have a 20 percent or greater differentiation between one category and another, you've got a valid indication that the higher category is what you prefer.

Chapter 6

Universal Breakpoints
The "Top 10"

Capsule Summary

Some events signaling a breakpoint are very basic. Some are more subtle, and will vary from one career stage to the next. In this chapter, we'll describe the most common breakpoints—those we call the "Top 10"—which tend to cut across all career stages.

Even though events that signal these breakpoints can be basic, basics are very important and we've found that some people still choose to ignore them. Head in the sand, they refuse to address change. Or they pretend that changes will happen to someone else, but not to them.

People who do recognize the importance of these "leading indicators," however, are forewarned and able to capitalize on many otherwise overlooked career opportunities.

BREAKPOINT 1: A CHANCE TO MOVE

Here's the most obvious breakpoint. You're offered a change—to a new location, new company, new position. The ball's in your court and opportunity's beckoning—or so it seems.

But the choice is never simple. The stories you hear about the couple who find their fortune after they decide on a whim to move across country are apocryphal. Though the analogy's not exact, a more apt description is the axiom "Marry in haste, repent in leisure."

Breakpoint Signals

Jim got the call on a Wednesday morning. His college economics professor and faculty adviser—who'd kept in touch during the past ten years—was on the phone with a "ground floor" offer. A new concept in sales of a consumer product we'll call Sherlock Pet Collars—to use, instead of the traditional pet-store outlets, a door-to-door, direct sales, neighborhood club approach never before tried for pet products. Jim's job was to hire individual salesmen on commission in towns across the country.

Jim had the background and expertise to set up these sales networks. He'd been with a successful encyclopedia sales firm for six years. The skills were in place, his former adviser told him. The move was a natural.

Jim bit the lure hard enough to fly from his New York area home to Houston to meet the CEO of the new organization. The company had talked with his former adviser, who was coming on as vice-president of sales. Jim would be general sales manager for the entire eastern territory. Everything on his side of the Mississippi would be his responsibility. The first years would be tough—setting up the sales network throughout the country—and Jim would have more travel time than he'd grown accustomed to. But the rewards looked dazzling. There was ownership—a 15 percent share in the company after only ten years through a stock-option plan and an automatic 1 percent share to begin with. The rest of the fringe-benefits package was equally tempting. A full health and retirement plan—full use of a company Lincoln Continental—and a luxurious office suite, part of the plush quarters that took up two floors in a soaring steel-and-glass contemporary skyscraper in downtown Houston.

As a final sweetener, the new CEO offered a lock-in mortgage with the Houston bank that was the company's primary lender. With the proceeds from only a break-even sale of his house in New York, Jim would have an easy purchase of a posh Houston suburban estate with swimming pool, tennis court, and easy monthly payments.

It wasn't long before Jim's wife was in the Houston area looking at houses. The company's generous salary package was the final convincer, along with a five-year contract that called for small automatic increases that grew as sales objectives were met.

"The whole thing seemed like a sure bet," Jim recalls. "We had the contract, we had the house, we had the car—nothing could go wrong."

Alas, the future proved otherwise. Jim worked constantly, straining his marriage and family relationships, to set up "one of the finest sales teams in the country—I still believe that." The product sales in Jim's region were outstanding that summer—in the areas where he'd had the opportunity to get men and women in place. The fall season results in the Northeast dropped, of course, but remained strong in the South.

Problem was, the sales in the other half of the country didn't come close to meeting expectations. The revenue stream that the new corporation had counted on to service its initial debt just wasn't there.

Jim had made a point of asking the CEO, during their initial series of interviews, about this very contingency. "No problem," the CEO assured him. Jim's former adviser added more comforting information. They had the financing in place for the long term. The Houston bank officer was a personal friend of the CEO. Nothing could go wrong.

Regrettably, the note the new corporation had signed was a demand note. The Houston bank that was the new company's primary lender was closely allied to a number of oil-exploration firms. When the price of oil dropped and sent Houston into an economic tailspin, the bank was "forced" to call the loan on Jim's company, despite the personal friendship between the lending officer and the CEO.

The result? "Sherlock Pet Collars went bankrupt in its second year," Jim recalls with a trace of bitterness. "All the contacts I'd made, all the commitments I'd taken, all the lives I'd touched as I put my team together . . ." His voice trails off and he turns up an empty palm. "And now I'm here in Houston with a house to sell in a rock-bottom real estate market before the bank forecloses. If I'm lucky I can get a fifth of my down payment back."

He doesn't mention the prospect of moving again—the Houston economy being what it is, he didn't have a prayer of getting a comparable job in the Houston area. So he and his wife are packing once more, to move to a rented house. The consolation is that the new job—also with a start-up company—is in the Northeast, where chances of an economic slump are less likely.

Breakpoint Forces

Jim's story, regrettably, isn't unique. With every chance to move, there are accompanying risks, some obvious and some hidden. Some—like the risk of the oil-connected economic slump—may be beyond anyone's control, but should still be taken into account in a well-thought-out analysis of any new opportunity.

Other risks—like the demand note that was the key underpinning of the new company's financing—could have been uncovered if Jim had pressed. Instead he took the word of his former mentor that all was secure —a tempting move and one that's easily rationalized, but dangerous just the same.

What makes us ignore these risks? We're all creatures of hope. Many of us are eager for greener pastures and new opportunities. When one comes, we may be reluctant to investigate fully, unwilling to risk spoiling our dream. Or we may be fearful of delay, rationalizing that if we wait to analyze the situation, the opportunity may vanish.

BREAKPOINT STRATEGY: THE RATING CHART

Get your ideas on paper—*before* you have a chance to move. Writing your ideas in advance will make you more aware of risks you might otherwise ignore. And if you prepare the chart we recommend, you'll be able to reach an evaluation quickly, minimizing risks that go with delay. The categories are weighted by the values you give them. Once you've added them up, you know how you feel about the move.

The chart we recommend has four categories: region, industry, company, and people. You evaluate these categories using a simple numbered scale to respond to predictions about each one. For each, you score your new opportunity as follows: If the new position looks better than where you are now, score a +1 to +5 depending on how much better. If the new position looks the same, score 0. If it looks worse, score −1 to −5. We've provided a sample list of predictions that should be adequate, but you should add your own to reflect your preferences. Also, if one category is twice as important to you as another, double the points for that category.

When you've finished rating your predictions, add up the pluses and minuses. A high positive score indicates you should say "yes" to the move, while a low positive score indicates second thoughts are in order.

We recommend that you have your spouse and kids make the same kind of analysis for the categories that are important to them. We further recommend that you try to work their opinions into your planning as objectively as possible. If they know they're being consulted first and that their opinions are factored into the equation, whether or not they're valued at the same level as yours and your spouse's won't be so important. The value is established that their voices are heard and potential problems are uncovered.

SAMPLE RATING CHART

The Region
1. It's got the resources for the leisure-time activities that we want.
2. It's got the schools we want.
3. The economy is strong in this region.
4. The region has other opportunities in my area.
5. The cost of living is reduced from where we are now.
6. My new salary and benefits will offset any increased cost of living, even after moving costs and home sale and purchase.
7. The area has the shopping facilities we want, conveniently located.
8. Any special services our family needs (special education, special medical) are conveniently available in the new location.

The Industry
1. My new position is in an expanding industry.
2. My new position is in a relatively stable industry, where the start-up and shut-down patterns are not volatile.
3. The region we're moving to is "where it's at" in the industry.

The Company
1. The company (or the branch) I'll be joining is new and needs the results I can provide: immediate sales, immediate production.
2. The company (or the branch) I'll be joining is well on its way, so it needs my administrative and organizational skills.
3. The company (or the branch) I'll be joining has been established for nearly a decade. My administrative skills will fit right in, and I know I'll be well liked by those who work with me.
4. The company (or the branch) I'll be joining has been around long enough to become stale. My administrative skills would get me by, but I see a real opportunity to turn the company around with my performance skills and my leadership ability to inspire fresh enthusiasm.

5. The CEO of the new company has a good record and is at least five years from retirement.
6. The company's position in the industry requires that it emphasize my area of professional expertise. (If you're a fast-track candidate, a "yes" answer to this question is good for you. If you're a steady-path candidate, the reverse is true.)

The People

1. The people I'll be working with are "my type."
2. The people who will be supervising me are "my type."
3. I can see vacancies developing at the level above me within the next two years, and the company promotes from within to manage those levels.
4. I've had a chance to get acquainted with each of the people who will have a say in my future and who will evaluate my performance.

This last point is especially important in a small company, as a client we'll call Sherry Victor learned to her regret. Interviewing for an unadvertised accountant's position at a one-year-old firm, she met with the president of the company and was very taken with the company's prospects. It had some great deals going and was in dire need of her strong accounting skills to get the company organized for the expansion that the president had in mind. "I'd like you to meet our vice-president of marketing and our vice-president of operations," the president told her. "I wouldn't do anything without their approval, of course you understand."

Sherry met one of the vice-presidents and was convinced they had hit it off. The meeting with the other vice-president was to be arranged through the president's office, but it just didn't happen. The president called back the next week. "Look, I just haven't been able to schedule that second meeting," he said, "but we're in a position to make you the offer. Can you come aboard by the first of the month?"

Thrilled, Sherry said yes. But later she had cause to regret the move. Though her skills were a perfect match for the new firm, the one executive she hadn't met turned out to be the primary "consumer" of her services. The spread sheets and property analyses he demanded were the firm's "bread and butter" work. The work that the president and the marketing chief wanted, it turned out, was mostly managing their personal financial planning. The financial analyses of the company's deals were the province of the one executive she hadn't met.

To make a long story short, there was a personality clash between Sherry and her "immediate supervisor." There was also a strong political clash between him and the president. Sherry had been hired without his knowledge. He had planned to bring on a bookkeeper from his personal accountant's firm and to use that firm to handle the company's more sophisticated accounting needs. The president had other ideas. Wanting someone like Sherry "in house"—and because he hadn't wanted to risk a conflict in the decision-making process—he'd presented the EVP with a fait accompli, Sherry's appearance at work.

The EVP was too valuable to the company to be treated in this manner, and he knew it. He refused to recognize Sherry's talents. Nothing Sherry could produce was done to his satisfaction. His hostile eye picked up every typographical error—even on first drafts that weren't meant for him to see. He criticized letter-perfect reports because he didn't like the "layout." If the layout was exactly as he'd asked for it, he'd find something else that was wrong. Some category wasn't broken out properly, or another category wasn't included, or the type of graph wasn't clear enough. If all else failed, he'd say that the report took too long to produce and that any competent bookkeeper could have done the same in half the time.

Sherry rose to the challenge, of course. She performed better and better. She'd been a star at her previous accounting firm, and she didn't intend to let a political clash between two superiors overshadow what her talents could achieve. For nearly a year, she worked extra hours. She calculated that the work product she produced would have cost the company nearly ten times her salary if they'd used an outside firm such as the EVP had planned to do. Moreover, she was careful to maintain good relations with the president and the VP of marketing, working evenings and weekends doing their personal financial records, tax returns, and the like.

But her efforts were to no avail. One week at the end of the year, the EVP was out of the office from Monday through Wednesday. Sherry assumed that he was on a business trip, but didn't ask where. That Wednesday afternoon, the president called her into his office and told her the news. The EVP had refused to come to work until Sherry was no longer working for the company. "It was him or me," she recalls. "That's how he put it to the president, and when the choice came down to that, what was fair to me wasn't as important as the value the EVP had to the company. The EVP was primary income producer. The deals he made and the financing he got was what put meat on the table. I was staff, he was line, and the president really didn't have a choice."

Is there a moral to Sherry's story? Of course. You've got to meet all your supervisors. Find out where you'll be on the organization chart and who will be a "consumer" of your product within the office. Then insist on a meeting with each of those people who'll be important to your future. If a "scheduling difficulty" comes up, be open about the situation. Say you aren't prepared to come to the company until you're certain you'll have the right "chemistry" with each of those you'll be working for. After all, your boss is your key to success. Aside from hiring you, your boss will train you, provide favorable (or unfavorable) press about you to management, give you raises, provide promotion opportunity, and, perhaps, serve as a reference should you decide to leave the company. This kind of reasonable request won't *jeopardize* the offer, unless, like the company Sherry joined, the new firm has a conflict that someone's trying to hide.

Remember, when evaluating opportunities, there is always attendant risk. How you evaluate risks or negatives may be just as important to your success quotient as the obvious benefits.

BREAKPOINT 2: A COMMAND CHANGE

A vice-president at a major auto-leasing company, Steve was elated when he and other department heads met the new president. "Don't bother me with details," the new man said. "Just keep me posted." Steve was independent by nature, and those orders were just what he wanted to hear. He kept on doing what he knew was an excellent job. He submitted weekly reports that presented the company's financial picture in clear, professional terms. But within six months, Steve was shocked to learn he'd been slated for termination.

What happened? Steve missed two key *breakpoint signals*. First, the background of the new boss wasn't in Steve's field—a fact Steve knew but didn't fully appreciate. With a background in marketing, the new president couldn't quite master the accountant's professional reports that had suited Steve's former boss so well. But the new man wasn't about to let Steve know he needed help.

The second tip-off was the vague, general order: "Just keep me posted." The new boss had been vague purposefully, to avoid taking over in dictatorial fashion. But he didn't expect to be taken so literally. Other department heads were wise enough to test his meaning with frequent informal contacts. While they were getting closer to the new president, Steve was becoming "the forgotten man."

Breakpoint Forces

The closer your job to the new boss, the more inevitable that your job will change with change in command. Either you'll change the way you operate to suit the boss, or someone will replace you. Why? Because your boss's background and individual "chemistry" are different from those of your previous boss, and because each boss must take some actions to reassure superiors (and maybe even self) that command has been firmly established. Remember, *your boss's* job is on the line too, and personal loyalty and "chemistry" are most important factors in career success. The pattern's usually the same. The new boss comes in reassuring people that there are no plans to make "significant" changes. But sooner or later, heads roll.

Breakpoint Strategy

Find out what's wanted and provide it on a timely basis—when and how the new boss prefers. Check for clarity and understanding periodically to see how you're doing.

BREAKPOINT 3: AN EVALUATION-SIGNAL CHANGE

Breakpoint Signals

Bill was a mid-level strategic-planning director at a major paper-manufacturing company. He'd been consistently turning in superior performance, and knew he was first among four contenders for the next opening at the general manager level. The spot he wanted most was the general manager position running the southeastern division, and he'd been told that he "had the best shot" for that post, in part because the plant was located in Bill's home state.

But when the southeastern division manager announced his retirement, the man picked to replace him wasn't Bill. What particularly disturbed Bill was that the man who got the position wasn't as well qualified.

"We've got bigger and better things in mind for you," Bill's boss told him. "Not to worry." The company would take care of Bill in the future.

But would they? The key unknown—an unknown too important to be left to fate and trust and reassurance. When Bill came to us we told him he was at a breakpoint and should take immediate steps.

Other evaluation signals are just as direct and just as important as being passed over for a promotion. Two critical signals in this area are a missed raise and negative performance evaluation.

Do these sound too obvious? Impossible to overlook? Perhaps they are. But too frequently these signals *aren't* obvious. They're frequently hidden —masked by a boss's positive presentation that says, "Not to worry." Alternatively, your boss may avoid sending a negative signal altogether.

Breakpoint Forces

No boss wants to "turn off" an employee with discouraging words about the employee's performance. Very few managers will say, "You were passed over for the promotion because we thought John Smith would do a better job" or, "You didn't get the raise because we don't think you have a future here, and we aren't willing to spend the additional dollars to keep you."

At an evaluation conference, few bosses, particularly if newly hired, will say, "You're not doing very well, and if you don't improve in these four specific areas, you'll be fired."

What you hear instead are oftentimes well-meaning—but ill-advised and ultimately unfair—attempts to smooth over and sugar-coat bad news.

Often if you're passed over for promotion it's because "we have bigger and better things in mind for you." Or "It's because John was most senior; your turn will come." Or "We had to take Jim's special relationship with the directors into account."

If you didn't get a raise, you may hear, "I just couldn't get the chief to put it in the budget this year." Or "Everybody's taking a beating this year." Or "We're lucky we all didn't have to take pay cuts this year."

The criticism you need to hear at your evaluation conference may be masked by "We think you're doing a super job. There are just a couple minor details you might think of to get that extra polish to come up from a 99 to 100."

Why do bosses go to such lengths to sugar-coat? They're faced with a management dilemma. They want to motivate you to keep working and do not need trouble. In addition, aside from motivational needs that each boss perceives, bosses may try to jolly you along because criticism and conflict make *them* uncomfortable. All too frequently, the boss tries to promote a "team" or "family" atmosphere where everyone is friendly, and where the boss is the supportive, nurturing coach or parent type. Depending upon personality, he or she may directly avoid criticizing your performance, not because the need for criticism isn't apparent, but because it's simply another unpleasant task to put off until another day.

Breakpoint Strategy

How do you handle this reluctance to disclose the true state of affairs? With slow, patient persistence and tact. Ask, "Where do you see me in the next four or five years here at the company?" Odds are, you'll get the reply: "I definitely see you getting promoted. You're doing a fine job and we here at Perennial Papers, Inc., believe in promoting from within."

All too frequently, you'll feel an initial surge of reassurance, and shuffle away with a grin and a smile, thanking your boss for the words of praise. However, when you stop to think about it, you'll realize the boss hasn't really told you anything.

When you get a general affirmative reply such as the one we've just described, ask, "Could you be a bit more specific?" or "Could you expand on that a bit?" You're looking to establish the true state of affairs—what your boss really sees in your future with positions and dates of promotion. You won't get the full picture, of course, so do not persist and persist. In the first place, your boss—unless the sole owner of the company—won't have authority to state with assurance just when and how your next promotion will come. Second, your boss may not have thought about the matter. Your questions will get that thought process started, and to alert your boss to your attitude—that you'll not be content to keep your nose patiently buried in your work until the company's whim and caprice should chance to favor you.

Be sure you ask these questions with tact, however, to avoid giving the appearance of being overdemanding or laying down an ultimatum. No boss likes to be backed into a corner. When you ask the questions, keep your eyes and ears open for signals that the reassuring words may not be what they seem. In a face-to-face meeting, if you're alert you can tell when the signals are mixed or you're not getting the full story. That's your immediate indicator. You'd better activate your résumé and seek opportunities elsewhere while you continue to work.

BREAKPOINT 4: A CHANGE IN COMPANY NEEDS

About five years ago, the president of a leading manufacturer of floor covering came to me and discussed his desire to reorient the thrust of the business. He felt that the company had suffered of late by not remaining current in its approach to consumer markets. Though the company had built a powerful distribution system, the president saw the need for heightening consumer awareness in a product category which had over the years become almost generic in nature. He felt that some new blood would help.

After an exhaustive search of five to six months, a well-qualified executive was hired and told, "Take charge. Do what you feel is in the best interest of the company, and I'll support your effort." After a number of months, the new executive was doing a good job in the consumer-awareness areas, but was substantially ignoring the strong base upon which the company had been built, the distributor network. The president began to subtly suggest that perhaps more travel was needed to gain market insight and stay current with what had been happening in the field. He was reminded by his new exec that things were changing and the new course was the right way to go.

After about three years, the company found itself with a neglected distributor network and an eroding market share. The new executive was told that things were not working out.

Breakpoint Signals

The bad news came as a great shock to the executive, who felt that real headway was being made. He had missed a critical tip-off from the president. The company needs had changed. The once powerful distribution network now needed attention. By failing to recognize the change, the executive missed the chance to continue leadership, and lost his job.

Breakpoint Forces

The worth of your skills to the company depends on your company's needs—now. To cite another example, with a technology background you could have risen quickly in cable TV a decade ago. Technological advances were what the industry needed back then. Later, marketing and raising capital became important as the companies expanded. Today, engineering, productivity, and marketing expertise are needed, as cable companies compete and attempt to quickly deliver the installations they've promised, which maximize profits.

Meanwhile, the auto industry in Detroit is looking for technology experts, having concentrated too long on marketing and style or what they thought the consumer wanted.

Your company too may have changing needs based on recent history, as with the floor-covering company we've just discussed, or due to technological changes in the market. As a general rule, a firm that's expanded production too quickly and now needs to consolidate isn't the best place for a marketing person to move up.

Breakpoint Strategy

Try to look at your company's needs from the CEO's point of view. Where do you fit in? As we've said, before, if you want major leadership responsibility, match your background with a company that needs your skills and abilities for its core business. But if you want stability, look for a company where your particular function may not be so crucial.

BREAKPOINT 5: A CHANGE IN YOUR PRODUCTIVITY/ SKILL QUOTIENT

Breakpoint Signals

I recall a manager at Procter & Gamble who was noted for his ability to deliver—and also for his ability to chew up subordinates in the process. Rather than leaving the executive in a broad role where he had functioned effectively for more than a dozen years, the company moved him to a very specialized job in a newly acquired division, where his effect on his subordinates wouldn't be detrimental. The result for the company was a highly competent executive performing well in the area of his greatest competence.

For the executive, however, the result was a terminal job. If he had the potential to move up, it was unrecognized. The company made its decision, put him in his pigeonhole, and forgot him. He would be unable to move up unless he left the company. Why? Because the company had changed his assignment to a no-growth position. In analytical terms, his productivity/skill quotient was not close to 100 percent. And the company had decided he wasn't capable of handling a position where he had less than total mastery of the job and people.

Sometimes, you can be pushed into positions where your productivity/skill quotient is too low—through no fault of your own. In the 1960s, for example, the Scott Paper Company embarked on a program to "strengthen" management ranks. The reasoning was that if top management was well grounded in several disciplines, the company would be better managed overall. During the next ten years, excellent managers were promoted out of areas where they had been successful into new jobs. Top sales managers were moved into production, top production people into sales, etc. What ensued was, if not a travesty, certainly a weakening of both company resources and executive development.

Not only did the company lose the benefit of outstanding sales, marketing, and production talent on an everyday operating basis; it led managers away from strength, creating mismatched confusion in the executive ranks and causing many frustrated managers to pursue careers elsewhere.

To date, the company has not regained its former top ranking in the field of paper products. It's still struggling to remain competitive, while Kimberly-Clark and others leading to strength have outflanked Scott in many product categories.

Rarely does such career mismatching occur company-wide as a result of policy, however. More likely it's ambition that drives managers beyond the work-load or skills level they're ready for. When you've exceeded your productivity/skill limits in a particular job that you've actively sought, you become more overburdened and stressed than if your assignment had been changed simply to broaden your capabilities. At this point, though you may feel like you're properly overachieving and that you'll soon get your bearings, you're in danger. You may only need time to get some more experience or training, but your superiors may conclude that you're incompetent, that you've exceeded the limits made famous by Dr. Lawrence

Peter in his book *The Peter Principle*. If they do, you may not be left in your mismatched spot much longer.

Over time, the stresses of a low productivity/skill quotient make themselves felt in another career danger—the symptoms of "burnout." The typical burnout pattern occurs when the productivity/skill quotient has been low over a prolonged period, in a series of positions where you haven't come close to mastering the skills required. Because you've been sprinting to catch up at work too long, you've neglected the rest of your life. Painful non-work needs make themselves felt. You notice disenchantment. You drag—even when you've had enough sleep and physical exercise. The same tasks take more energy and the new ideas just won't come. You feel guilty when leaving your job—even after a full day's work. You have trouble making decisions. You have confrontations with people either on the job or at home. You're suspicious of those around you—perhaps even with friends. You find that insignificant disappointments or setbacks cause you undue depression and anger. You try to hide the symptoms, but your superiors will notice.

Alternatively, as in our earlier examples, you may become ultraproficient at your work, only to be taken for granted by your superiors. This career hazard can make you a forgotten person, and it's doubly dangerous. While you may think you should be able to work without more recognition than you're getting, you may *need* more recognition than you're getting—to avoid giving your superiors the impression that you lack the potential for promotion or for adequate compensation.

I recall a conversation with a senior executive at American Express a few years ago. Her concern was that she had become so indispensable in her job that top management would not promote her further. This is a common problem for highly conscientious people who either do everything themselves or develop special skills that are difficult to find in others.

Breakpoint Forces

A time-honored rule is that if you've got a lot to learn about your present job, you're not ready to move. Of course, this rule presupposes that you and your job are well suited for each other—otherwise your lack of mastery may be a good reason for you to bail out.

Balance is important at this point. A year or so ago, we were working on a search for a large manufacturer of high-tech products. Because of the newness of the industry and the need the company expressed for a top-flight manager, we experienced difficulty locating a person who had been on any job long enough to measure progress. Because the industry was growing so rapidly, competent managers were moved very quickly through the system, in many cases so quickly that measuring success and long-term ability was impossible.

What we're concerned about here, however, is the point at which you do reach mastery over your job. Since your learning curve has flattened, the odds are that you'll become bored, as Ed was bored with Regal Sceptre, or too comfortable. Or, even if you don't feel you're in a rut (or a comfortable groove), your superiors may. In either case, you're at a breakpoint. Change is more likely than not.

Change is also impelled by how your performance compares with that of your peers. If you're at the top or the bottom of the achievement list, you know you're at a breakpoint.

Breakpoint Strategy

A good first step toward finding out where you stand is to use a short exercise I developed a few years ago when I received a number of calls from executives at the General Mills Company asking for career guidance. I'm not certain why these calls were grouped as they were, but after the second or third call, it became clear that these individuals needed a base or perspective point from which to measure their career progress. At General Mills they lacked management exposure with other companies, and were somewhat hampered by geographic isolation. The executives had no base from which to measure success. As we've stated before, one of the first rules one learns in basic navigation is that you must attempt to determine where you are before making course corrections.

And so in this case we simply recommended no action. We told the executives simply to take inventory. They listed the goals they had for their jobs and put the lists away for six months. Then they called again and we checked their career progress against the goals they'd set.

By holding off on a decision for six months, we were able to help the executives develop a trend line against which to compare and develop future goals.

What gets you out of burnout or out of the other career traps we've just discussed? The first step is to recognize that you're having serious difficulties and to decide you've got to make a career move. The second step is knowing where you want to be on your career chart and what the next logical step should be. We've provided the framework for you to get your bearings in our two "Test Yourself" chapters. Also, in the following chapters on the separate career phases, you'll find our recommended strategies as well as the stories of a number of G&S clients who fought their way back on track.

BREAKPOINT 6: YOUR RISK QUOTIENT CHANGES

Breakpoint Signals

I recall a time at the Ralston Purina Company in the early to mid-1970s when top management was committed to growth in the form of diversifying their existing business, which consisted primarily of cereal products for people and animals.

One area they approached enthusiastically was a new concept in prepared-food marketing. The idea was to set up chicken fast-food stands in grocery stores. The concept had merit. With a greater number of working couples shopping after work, it seemed logical that they would be happy to stop at the stand and take a bucket of fresh chicken home for dinner.

Several key managers in the company sought the opportunity to run this new area and one was selected. To make a long story short, the business never took off, and neither did several key people running it.

I recall another incident, this one with Gillette, during the same period. With a booming consumer interest in houseplants, Gillette decided to cash in. They formed a plant-care division to sell, feed, spray, and display plants. They bought a number of small companies manufacturing specialized products and were off and running.

Shortly after they hired a bright young executive from a consulting company to run the business, I received a call from an executive in the personal-care division. He was very unhappy that he had not been given an opportunity to run the plant-care project and felt that his not being asked represented lack of confidence from Gillette's executive then in charge of the group.

When we talked further, he admitted that, yes, he had been given a good deal of responsibility in personal care, and yes, he did have a new product of his own. From what he said, it made sense for him to stay on rather than to look elsewhere. In time, the plant-care division either died or was sold off or both, and his new shampoo product in personal care turned out to be one of the most successful new items to hit the market that decade. His own career success was in direct proportion to that of the product he had decided to stay with and build.

Breakpoint Forces

Trouble is opportunity, as the saying goes. When you see the opportunity to take on a risky assignment, or when you have one thrust upon you, remember that this cuts two ways and evaluate risk factors carefully. As well as providing you with an opportunity to hit a home run and move up, trouble also provides your superiors with the opportunity to protect themselves, if they make you the scapegoat and move you out.

Breakpoint Strategy

Don't let your good judgment be consumed by confidence. Be sure your skills quotient has reached the comfort point *before* you take on an optional risk.

BREAKPOINT 7: YOU COMPLETE A COMPANY "CYCLE"

Breakpoint Signals

Several years ago AT&T launched their Initial Management Development Program—a "sink or swim" training program to give young managers the opportunity for immediate experience managing line workers in the company's long-distance toll and information offices, installation, business offices, and plant and construction. The task of managing mature, union-oriented workers as a first assignment was daunting to some, but highly stimulating to others. One IMDP in particular, I recall, had rave reviews for the way he'd taken charge of his group of construction workers. He, too, was more than pleased with his work assignment. In fact, he made it known to his superiors that he wanted to stay in the construction end of the business and that he was looking forward to moving up to his boss's position of district construction manager.

The fly in the ointment was the company policy of rotation between "line" and "staff" positions. After two or three years "in the field," the pattern had been to assign the manager to the home office for a minimal one-year stint on the staff. Our IMDP let it be known that he wasn't a "white-collar-oriented" kind of guy and that he didn't see how a "year or so pushing a pencil behind some desk in Newark" would aid his development.

The result? Remember, he was a highly successful and highly valued manager in his present spot. The company kept him at that level for six years rather than the usual three, and his pay raises suffered as a result. At the end of the sixth year, he was formally offered his choice: either take the staff position in Newark or leave the company. Having matured a bit as he watched his fellow IMDPs move up the ladder while he remained behind, our man elected to go to Newark. His regret, however, was that he hadn't made the choice earlier, for he'd lost a good deal of ground by his attempt to buck the company-cycle program.

Breakpoint Forces

Your company may have an announced policy of rotating assignments. The changes may be based on job characteristics—say, from three years in a line position to two years on staff and then back into the field. Or maybe the change is to provide background in different geographic regions, or for exposure to the home-office "culture" for a year or two, particularly if you're in a foreign-owned company. If so, unless you've lost track of the calendar, you know when you're about to reach this kind of breakpoint.

The first problem here is that many company "rotation" policies are unannounced. They may be unwritten, just general principles in the minds of top management. The only way you'll spot this kind of breakpoint is to look for patterns in the careers of those above you.

The major problem here, though, is that the rotation "cycle" may not fit with your plans and goals. In the case of our IMDP, the cycle *did* fit his long-range goals, but his shortsighted orientation kept him from acknowledging this fact.

Breakpoint Strategy

The company will invariably say it's grooming you for bigger and better things. But the plan may or may not be right for you. It's up to you to plot your own career course, using the materials we've provided to decide whether you want to go with the company flow.

BREAKPOINT 8: YOUR VISIBILITY QUOTIENT CHANGES

When Natalie joined a Fortune 500 foods company, they were right in the middle of their annual United Fund drive. Natalie didn't take part, but she noticed that the company president headed up the fund-raising effort. During the next eleven months, she spent evenings and weekends lining up potential contributors, and then volunteered for a position as group leader in that year's fund drive. Guess whose group set an all-time company record for donations received? And guess who was promoted to a key position on the president's staff a month later?

Breakpoint Forces

The more people who see you work, the greater your opportunities to move up—and the greater the expectation that you'll produce something impressive. Keep in mind that "work" here means more than just your job assignment. Professional organizations, civic, political, and church groups all give you the opportunity to maximize your visibility.

We've found that when managerial and performance qualifications are about equal, style is viewed as *most important* to top managers who are required to spend considerable time in the public eye with the press, stockholders, or employees at functions or conventions.

Several years ago I met a fast-moving manager with IBM who told me that he had personally hired a PR firm to represent him. He claimed that his image was so improved within the company, and his promotions occurred so far in advance of his peers', that he had recouped the PR expense severalfold. More important, he was viewed as a leader and his performance was extolled throughout IBM.

Breakpoint Strategy

A key to making visibility work for your career is to be selective, to make certain your visibility has an impact.

BREAKPOINT 9: YOU GET "LEVERAGE"

What many execs tend to forget or ignore is the leverage they have gained by virtue of their present experience. Like money in the bank, this experience may have greater value when invested outside your present company.

Breakpoint Signals

If, for instance, you're in year three of a five-year track to a mid-level managerial job, give active consideration to what value this has outside your company. It is very possible that you could change to another fine company at one or two levels higher and significantly higher pay.

When you project this forward, you'll find that if you continued to progress in your new job and if you received 20 percent more to switch companies and 15 percent raises per year, you'd be way ahead. For example:

Present Track

Salary	$50,000	
Year 4	$57,500	raise of 15% = $ 7,500
Year 5	$66,125	raise of 15% = $ 8,625

New Company

Salary	$60,000	
Year 4	$69,000	raise of 15% = $ 9,000
Year 5	$79,350	raise of 15% = $10,350

Breakpoint Forces

In addition to obvious financial considerations, you'll find that you have had better exposure to top management during this time, and if you've done a good job, will probably be more valued. Also worth remembering, your new top management has not seen your previous mistakes as a trainee. They'll view you as the pro from XYZ company.

These financial and psychological factors are the foundation upon which the executive search business in the United States is built. They have the opportunities, you have the leverage.

Breakpoint Strategy

Your company has certain criteria for moving you to the next level. Whether the criteria have to do with your performance, or with your years on the job, your age, or your pay level, it's up to you to find out. Then find out what criteria other companies set for the level you're seeking. If you already meet those criteria, your position at your present company gives you "leverage" to move up more quickly than you'd thought possible.

But remember, any new situation has pitfalls. With opportunity comes risk. Do you want to chance a move?

About two years ago I had a long conversation with a senior manager at one of our client companies, Nabisco Brands. The manager had moved consistently forward and was well liked by the president, Ross Johnson. After one or two frustrating assignments and several more conversations, the manager told me he was anxious to leave and had in fact agreed to join a new company. I was surprised, for the new company was in a very different business with an unfamiliar channel of distribution to the consumer. I understand that after several years at the new company, things have not gone well.

Should he have stayed at Nabisco? That's anyone's guess, but the odds are good that he leveraged himself long-term into a weaker career pattern.

Study your career chart and our "chance to move" analysis method to evaluate the new company carefully against what you have.

BREAKPOINT 10: YOU REACH A PAY-SCALE PEAK OR BECOME MOST SENIOR

Lynda was 100 percent "comfortable" in her department manager's position at a major brokerage firm. The hours were right, department productivity had never been better, and after seven years on the job, her efficiency was superb. She had time for longer lunch hours and tennis three afternoons a week. Also, steady annual increases and bonuses she'd been getting through the years had made her personal lifestyle more comfortable. She was stunned when her boss told her that she was being replaced and that she could either take a job with more responsibility or resign from the firm.

Breakpoint Signals

What happened? First, Lynda looked to be enjoying too much leisure time. Though her productivity was as good as ever, she wasn't setting a good example for others at the office. Even though her boss wouldn't have told her *not* to take the leisure time, it rankled.

Second, and more important, Lynda was at the top of the pay scale for her position.

Breakpoint Forces

Pay differential is a primary force behind the "up or out" philosophy prevalent at many large companies. Either overtly or subtly, these companies encourage trainees to aspire to the president's job. They say that they want everyone to think of the "big picture" and that they plan work assignments to groom everyone to move up to his or her "fullest potential." But underneath the "reach for the stars" rhetoric is the cold, simple truth. If you've been on the same job for a number of years, they could fill your spot with a junior person at half the cost. So why should they let you keep garnering raises?

Since Lynda's laid-back work style rankled the boss, he had no reason to let her stay comfortable. While the captain of the football team may not be the best player on the field, he's usually at practice early, setting the pace.

Breakpoint Strategy

When you reach the top of the pay scale, you're at a danger point. Develop the contacts to allow you to move up or out *before* you reach the top of the pay scale.

Similar breakpoint forces are at work when you become most senior.

Breakpoint Signals

Remember the "up or out" philosophy. If this is the thinking at your company, you're at a breakpoint when you're the most senior worker at a particular level, or in your particular work assignment, whether you want to move or not.

Top management responds to seniority in different ways, not all constructively. In the early days of the development of the product management system, for example, high-powered young executives were sought from top graduate schools to work at companies like General Electric, Xerox, Procter & Gamble, and AT&T. For the most part, these grads started their careers at the same level. While the titles were different at various companies, ranging from marketing assistant to assistant product manager, the jobs were fairly consistent in content.

Over the next five or six years, the systems for accommodating these hard chargers ran smoothly. Then the inevitable question: What do we do with the very competent slower-track manager? General Foods Corporation, Colgate, and others added levels. Product managers deemed not ready to become group product managers were called senior product managers, and we now had our first look at promotion motivated by lack of confidence.

Breakpoint Forces

Yes, these "senior" people were performers. No, they weren't ready for much more responsibility now or perhaps ever. But the companies felt they had to do *something* with them, so they created stopgap positions which put off the inevitable. What next? Senior senior product managers?

Many other companies don't bother to create new layers. They simply terminate, reasoning that the high salary one senior employee draws can fund two or three talented less senior employees at the same level.

Breakpoint Strategy

How long was the previous senior person on the job? This may be one way to decide when to be ready to move to a less "up or out"-minded company.

But I wouldn't be too quick to rely on what others have done before you to establish your future plans. Work from your career chart, and keep the initiative whenever possible.

Chapter 7

The Trainee

Capsule Summary

When you and your "class" first sign onto a company payroll as trainees, you've probably been told what to expect. For one thing, your recruiters will have told you how long you'll probably spend as a trainee before getting your first "real" assignment. If there's a formal training program, your recruiters may also have mentioned certain specific performance criteria to be met before you "earn your wings."

Recruiters, however, very rarely mention some important performance criteria that can prevent you from earning your wings. As you'll see in this chapter, there are two sets of criteria: those everyone talks about and those hardly anyone mentions—to the trainee. You'll need to satisfy both to move up and away from the trainee phase. We call them "performance thresholds," because not until you've evidenced the required performance are you permitted to move on.

A TYPICAL STATED TRAINEE PERFORMANCE THRESHOLD

Orientation. You learn the company departments, branch offices, procedures, jargon. You get acquainted with company personnel.

Work Skills. You show satisfactory job-specific knowledge, along with general ability to write and speak with authority.

"Serving Time." You complete the required time period. This last may sound irrational. Why should Natalie, a dynamic Harvard M.B.A. who's memorized the company's international organization chart the first week, have to stay in the mailroom a moment longer? Hasn't she already shown what's required? The answer, of course, is that she hasn't shown what's really required. The company needs to know more about Natalie and her commitment before moving her up.

A TYPICAL UNSTATED TRAINEE PERFORMANCE THRESHOLD

Image. Looks, personality, motivation, character. Is the trainee a winner (i.e., "one of us")? Can he or she help our company/department/careers?

Loyalties. Will the trainee follow orders? Protect our company/department/careers?

The trainee is always at a breakpoint when the time period is complete. Before the time period is complete, the trainee will be at a breakpoint only when it appears that any of the *unstated* performance thresholds *won't* be met.

TRAINING PROGRAM: GENERAL BACKGROUND

On the surface, you enter what's called a "training program" to become familiar with the company's facilities and organization chart, to learn the jargon of whatever industry you're in, and to learn your company's particular methods of operation. Occasionally, you'll have tests to check your progress in these areas and make sure you're learning properly. You may also have tests asking about your attitudes, motivational drives, and career goals, with the reason given in semi-paternalistic phrases like "to help the company in second-tier placement" or "to assist the program director in recommending for future assignments." On the surface, it seems just like school, complete with a guidance department.

Don't believe it for a minute.

The unstated purpose of the training program is to pick up where the recruiting process left off. For the company, the purpose of the training period is simple: to identify winners and losers. At the end of the year, or however long your training period is designed to run, your "trainers" will be called upon to identify those who are "one of us" and those who aren't. Your class will be divided into three groups.

The rising stars will be marked quickly for second assignments where they'll be challenged.

Others will be given another chance to prove themselves.

The rest will be weeded out.

When training supervisors think of you or your work, the choice of winners and losers is always at the back of their minds. Always. Why? Because their careers may depend on the choices they make. If your boss sends you to the next level and you turn out to be a disappointment, who looks bad?

So after you've spent three sleepless nights working up your first report, he or she puts an arm around your shoulder and says, "God, I hated my first one of these. A real pain, right?"

You think the boss is being a friend and inviting you to blow off steam.

Maybe the boss even *wants* to be a friend and invite you to blow off steam.

But in the back of the mind is the question "Winner or loser?"

Guess which is the easier choice to make?

If your boss votes in your favor, your mistakes later on can come back to haunt. But if your boss votes against you, you're gone. And to superiors, the boss looks like a tough-minded executive not afraid to make the "difficult choice" for the good of the company.

Doctors get to bury their mistakes. Trainee supervisors get to "outplace" theirs.

BREAKPOINTS FOR A TRAINEE: THE PERFORMANCE THRESHOLD TESTS

Tests of your work skills, your image, and your loyalties are common to every stage of the career, and they occur so frequently that, in other stages, we wouldn't often think of them as career breakpoints unless someone of major importance was deliberately doing the testing. (In other career stages, your supervisors will be more preoccupied with meeting their work objectives than with testing you.) But in the trainee phase, you're on more tenuous ground. Since the major purpose of the trainee stage is to test recruits and weed out those who aren't "one of us," each point of testing can be a make-or-break item.

At the risk of appearing superficial, we begin with the most obvious point of testing, the most easily understood, and, paradoxically, the most frequently resisted.

"IMAGE" BREAKPOINT 1: DRESS CODE

Breakpoint Signal

Your boss (or someone else in the company who's in the know) says something like "We don't see too many plaid sport coats [or yellow shirts, or cowboy boots] around here."

Whenever you hear a comment about your dress that suggests it's out of line, take warning. You may have heretofore gloried in scorning stereotypes and scoffing at books such as *Dress for Success*. At college you may have taken great pride in dressing like a bum while you behaved like a genius. You may know millionaires who dress in baggy torn chinos and checked hunting shirts when they come into the office. The owner of your company, if it's small, may wear golfing clothes to work some days.

You, however, are neither millionaire nor company owner. And you're being paid to represent the company in more ways than the work you produce. Look around you. What do you see? What don't you see? Handle yourself accordingly.

Breakpoint Forces

The company needs to look better than its competitors ("better" means what your company management thinks is better). You're expected to do your part. Also, you're showing adherence to the company standards and rules—an outward expression of loyalty. It's like getting a haircut and donning a uniform your first day in boot camp.

Breakpoint Strategy

No ifs, ands, or buts. Invest in a good, tasteful, not necessarily expensive, wardrobe and stick to it.

What's good? Here you have a fine line between "now" and "someday." Look around at the people in your department. Look at where you want to be. Check the annual reports in your industry and compare photos of your company's top management with those of your company's two chief competitors. In many cases, you'll find a clear contrast between the "uniforms" worn by your team and the uniforms worn by the opposition. Depending on your career goal, perhaps you'll buy the same style suit as your company's EVP, but a less expensive brand. Ditto for shirts and shoes and ties. If you're a man, you won't look out of place if you're in the construction department, because you'll keep your jacket on a hanger and you'll turn up your sleeves. If you're female, you'll dress as formally as the best-dressed woman (or man if there isn't a woman) in upper management, because you'll at all times want to visually differentiate yourself from the secretaries.

Expensive? Yes, but consider the cost of the raises you could miss. If you don't look like a "comer" you won't be perceived as a comer.

WARNING ONE: Don't try the reverse-psychology trick of dressing in rags to appear in need of a raise. You won't generate sympathy, and you'll generate animosity for making the company look shoddy. People generally relate best to attractive, well-groomed, well-dressed people.

WARNING TWO: If your manner of dressing is too expensive, your boss may resent you. We know one young female trainee who scrimped and saved to buy all her things at Gucci and Saks. Result? Her bosses felt "outclassed"—thought she must have family wealth and therefore didn't need a raise. To make matters worse, management several levels up commented consistently about how well she dressed.

WARNING THREE: Be sure that whatever style you choose is one you're comfortable with. A young man we know thought smoking a pipe at his first evaluation conference would show his pipe-smoking boss a slightly older, more experienced image. At first it worked. After a few convivial moments of pipe filling, however, our friend pulled out his butane lighter, leaned forward, and proceeded to light up. But the flame, unbeknownst to him, was adjustable. He flicked the switch to turn it on, and the flames leaped up and set his forelock on fire. The boss, thinking quickly, grabbed the pitcher of water he always kept on the corner of his desk and drowned the flames. As you might imagine, there's no graceful way to recover from setting yourself afire in your boss's office. The young trainee—who immediately became an ex-pipe smoker—was not long for that job.

"IMAGE" BREAKPOINT 2: THE RIGHT STUFF

It may sound hopelessly superficial to speak of personality, motivation, and character as part of your "image." Regrettably, however, this is the way of things. No one has the time, and few have the training, to discover the essential person hidden beneath a trainee's charmingly juvenile façade. The probings your superiors make will be predictable and readily understood (after all, your boss may be called upon to recount them to his or her superiors). The conclusions your boss draws may depend not on the essential you, but on the image you decide to project.

Two common tests:

The "gofer" test. "Take this report down to photocopying, will you, Jim?" Or "Going out to lunch? Can you bring me back a pack of Camel Lights?" The trait being probed here is: Will the trainee recognize authority? Beneath the surface are also tests of the trainee's self-image and self-loyalty, since the task is somewhat demeaning, at least in comparison with what the trainee is ostensibly being paid to do.

Breakpoint Forces

The company and your boss both need to show who's in command. Conversely, neither the company nor your boss (except in aberrational cases) wants you to be a lackey. You're not being trained for that.

Breakpoint Strategy

Avoid refusal or direct conflict. But do make good-humored comments ("I think I can handle that, sir") that indirectly indicate you don't see yourself in the role of personal servant.

The "lost evening/weekend" test. Typically given at four-thirty and consisting of a project that has to be done by the following morning/ Monday, and will probably take just about that long to complete. Does the trainee have the commitment, stamina, and character to work hard without complaining?

Breakpoint Forces

The company needs people who will make sacrifices when required. Conversely, for reasons of both productivity and public relations, very few companies favor the complete workaholic. Most recognize that you need a life outside the office, and encourage it.

Breakpoint Strategy

Avoid refusal. Also avoid mention of the date or weekend you'll be giving up. But if there's a sacrifice on your part, discreetly allow cancellation of your plans to be overheard or learned of after the fact.

Other tests of your manners and values occur less frequently and deliberately, but they can be deadly serious. Some bosses have been known to take their trainee assistants out and deliberately put pressure on—to drink to excess, find call girls, whatever. As we discussed before, this is not only limited to the trainee. Some bosses will like the trainee more for succumbing to temptation (recall Hemingway, who said he never could trust a man who didn't drink). Others will hold the episode against you.

Even innocent misjudgments hurt. I was recently talking with an executive of a large insurance company who recounted an unfortunate incident. It seems that at a company party a senior executive drank a bit too much. One of his key managers (a woman), recognizing the danger involved, drove him home, a considerable distance from the office and in the opposite direction from her own home. After dropping him and his car off, she took a cab at her own expense to her home, arriving late and missing a dinner party.

The following Monday, when she half expected a quiet thanks, she was shocked to find her boss cold and aloof. The relationship deteriorated and she finally left the company.

Where had she gone wrong? Being driven home drunk by a young female manager was not the image her boss (or the boss's wife) wished to project to the company.

She should have been more sensitive to perceptions. Given the choice again, I'd bet she would seek out a man to do the driving. Even then it's risky. Perhaps just calling him a cab would have l een best.

Breakpoint Strategy

How are you to find out what kind of behavior is expected of you? Tactfully ask those who've gone before, those you perceive to be winners. Be alert for other clues before an episode occurs. Decide in advance what kind of game plan you want to set for yourself. Establish your values, and stick to them. No sense working for a company where your promotions seem hollow because you've gone against your conscience. A good ploy when declining is to laugh it off. "You're testing me, right?" A sense of humor can be a wonderful tool when used properly to ease tension.

Note to women: If your boss is male, you may also have to face the unpleasant test of his making a romantic overture. No romance may be involved; it may simply be his way of trying to assert authority or to be liked, a highly charged situation where romance is almost certainly a poisoned fruit.

Breakpoint Forces

Time was when company romance was seriously frowned on. Employees were not permitted to date. If they made the mistake of getting serious about each other and decided to get married, one of them, most often the woman, was forced to leave the company. This primarily occurred when a company romance usually involved an executive and secretary, and the presumption was that romance interfered with efficiency and loyalty.

Now, company romances are gaining greater acceptance. Increasingly, more women are in management positions and are thrown into proximity with men at meetings, conferences, business trips, etc. So, people being people, romance sometimes follows. Companies that previously frowned on such romances are now being forced to either accept them or lose two good people. Whether true or not, the press took great delight with the story of a romance between Bill Agee and Mary Cunningham at Bendix a few years ago.

The bottom line is that company loyalty and concern for company matters still must come first. Companies generally don't want to know who's sleeping with whom, who's living with whom. They want employee energies focused on company business.

Breakpoint Strategy

Though it may be difficult, particularly for a young single trainee, maintain separation of affairs of the heart and affairs of the office.

Tests of Your Work Skills. Obviously, these tests will vary from job to job, but there are some common criteria you'll be judged on. Here we present breakpoint strategies our clients have found helpful.

Breakpoint Strategies

A positive mental attitude is most important here.

• *Beat the deadlines.* Overdo the work rather than doing only what is asked. It's much easier to move ahead if you overdeliver at the outset of the job. This develops habits and patterns that will be useful as you move along.

• *Make it look easy.* In college, the "in" routine was to stay up all night before the test or the paper due date. Not so on the job. Nobody wants to see you gaunt, haggard, and sleepless at the end of the project. Your boss wants to see you bright, alert, and ready for a new assignment.

• *Find out what is expected of you.* Prodigious production does no good if it's misdirected. Discuss expectations with your superiors as soon as possible and develop a plan to measure progress in specific time blocks. Learn to check your priorities to do the most important things first.

• *Look around and see what "normal" work hours are for the rest of the company.* Be prepared to hear, "What time are you coming in tomorrow?" on a Friday afternoon. If so, schedule personal tasks with business tasks that day. You might plan a lunch in town with your spouse and some shopping or a show afterward. Other bosses have been known to say, "If my managers can't finish their work by five and still have time during the day for an hour or so of exercise, they're not organized well enough to work here."

• *Earn the backing of support staff; they can make or break you.* Your boss's opinion of you may be greatly influenced by opinions of clerical and secretarial staff. More importantly, these people have probably watched others in your situation make it or fail. If you treat them with proper courtesy and respect and a sense of humor, they're likely to be extremely valuable to you.

· *Work at good written communications.* If you're writing, make it simple. Use headings, summaries, "key concepts"—just as we've done here. Make your writing so easy to understand that the boss can grasp your main idea with just a quick glance or two. Also, remember that your "image" travels with whatever your name's on. Neatness counts! Most important, be accurate. Nothing will lose you ground faster than the boss's being embarrassed at a meeting because your numbers were off or a basic premise false. Check and recheck your facts. Avoid putting anything in writing you are not sure of.

· *Develop a professional attitude toward speaking and listening.* Many younger managers feel that they must speak and take control. You're there to learn and it's tough to learn when you're talking. Take the time to "preview" what you're about to say to people, especially your superiors, and try to present it in an organized fashion (e.g., "I see three problem areas here that we should address." Or "Let me tell you one critical advantage that this procedure should give us"). Also, be clear about instructions to secretaries. Don't be afraid to ask questions if you don't understand something.

Tests of Your Loyalties. You won't get out of the trainee phase unless you pass these. You're a trainee till you're "one of us."

The trick is to know just who "us" is.

At the trainee level, your loyalty to the company itself is generally taken for granted. At this stage, you don't know enough to be of much help to the competition, so management is not seriously concerned about whether you'd rather be elsewhere. Unless you're insensitive enough to be driving a new Datsun while you work for Chrysler, or chain-smoking Chesterfields while you work for R. J. Reynolds Co., you won't be likely to encounter much testing of your overall company loyalties.

On the other hand, you will be tested on your loyalty to the division or department and the people where you're first assigned.

Breakpoint Signal

Any sign of conflict between your group and another part of the company. Suppose your boss comes storming in with the next quarter's production quotas for your department. He shows you a page full of numbers and growls, "How can those idiots upstairs expect us to make these targets?"

Breakpoint Forces

First, remember that your boss may be putting on this display deliberately, especially if no one else is around. Whether or not the new quotas are fair or realistic may not be the real issue. The boss could just be giving you this opportunity to whine and pout to see what you do with it (a "right stuff" test). Or could be testing to see whether your instincts are to support implied judgments or to line up on the side of the supervisory staff. You should hope that your boss isn't really on the brink of a pitched battle with upper management. Such a conflict would only hurt both careers and detract from any recommendation of you that might be forthcoming.

Here the conflict is "vertical"—i.e., with a department that has supervisory powers over yours. If this conflict were openly expressed, it would be insubordination, a taboo in any organization.

Treatment of "lateral" conflicts, on the other hand, varies from company to company. The inevitable rivalries between departments and struggles for a bigger slice of the company's budget resources are more acceptable, and may even be encouraged by top management.

Point to Remember: Diverse interests within a company will inevitably lead to conflicts, and the way you handle those conflicts will be more and more important to your work as you move up. Learn to project different sets of loyalties: to the company as a whole, to the group you are currently in, and to the group you currently aspire to, more or less in that order. Play it straight and avoid being two-faced; by handling yourself with various groups you're showing leadership. And leadership, as you progress, is what more and more of your job will be about.

Breakpoint Strategy

As a trainee, how to respond to these conflicts? Take advantage of your position. You're not expected to have the answers, so don't offer opinions in highly charged areas. Rather, ask questions.

If it's your boss who's complaining, ask, "Did they stick it to any of the other departments?" "What's their rationale?" "How did we handle the last one of these?" "Do you want me to work up something on the changes we'll have to make?" Be understanding, supportive, and positive in your outlook.

If it's a fellow trainee complaining, or someone you may be called on to supervise, resist any temptations to become pals at the expense of the rest of the company. Steer clear of underground movements and budding revolutions. Emphasize commonality of interests. Ask questions to bring out the points benefiting both sides. Don't line up against either group, even if it's a departmental rivalry. The company may be planning to transfer you to the rival group next month.

Your advantage as a trainee: You're expected to have a distanced, less highly charged point of view. Your superiors may ask your opinion hoping to utilize that viewpoint—i.e., to see you as a consultant rather than an employee. Here is an opportunity to establish yourself with the authority of an "expert" (remembering the definition of an expert as "someone from more than five hundred miles away"). So utilize your training (e.g., "What Professor Kissinger always told us was . . .") and bring in some of the latest issues and business school techniques you're able to recall. *Caution:* Much of the time, however, your superiors will be utilizing your "consultant" mode to justify their own position and thinking. So don't be a show-off, especially if you're taking a contradictory stand. Avoid the common trainee error of always referring to "what we did or what they taught in graduate school."

Another advantage of being a trainee: You are expected to make some mistakes. Don't attempt to show that you're infallible; rather, show how you can learn from your mistakes and bail yourself out. What have your mistakes taught you about yourself? How can you correct them? What does the company need?

Your loyalty to your boss will also be tested. If you've put your boss in an unfavorable light, can you rectify things?

Breakpoint Signal 1

Your supervisor is a tough taskmaster, even unfair at times. His boss comes to your department for a late meeting and she takes the group out to dinner. Over drinks, you and she seem to hit it off. At a moment when the others can't hear, she quietly asks, "How do you like working with Mel?"

Breakpoint Signal 2

You've put in nearly a week of sixteen-hour days to finish a report. You hand the final draft to your boss's secretary for delivery to the typing pool. She glances up at you and remarks, "Mel drives me crazy with these things. I don't know how you can take working for that guy."

Breakpoint Forces

You're the newcomer. While both of these situations seem to invite an alliance against your boss, be wary of easily invited confidences. Both people have existing relationships with Mel. What he does in his position can affect each of them more than anything you can do in yours. Time for assumptions. First, assume that anything you say will eventually get back to Mel, and assume that Mel's supervisor likes the way Mel operates—or at least likes the results he produces.

Breakpoint Strategy

Turn the discussion away from any evaluation of your boss. Talk about your own progress instead, with remarks like "I'm getting a real education here" or "He's really showing me how to turn out the product." Show loyalty. Very rarely will you be pressed to give a negative evaluation of your boss. If you are faced with this rare situation, try to divert the discussion from evaluating your boss to suggesting new procedures or policies you would recommend to change things.

A more difficult situation exists if your boss has a serious personal problem that others in the company do not seem to recognize. Here blind loyalty would be a mark of bad judgment or disloyalty to the company. Example: You see your boss taking cocaine; or going to a motel with another employee. Unfortunately, your boss's failings may put you in a dangerous position. If your boss is caught after recommending you for advancement, his or her recommendation may be suspect. For you to make a direct report to his or her superior could be extremely dangerous, since you haven't the faintest idea whether the superior knows or has something equally damaging to hide that the boss knows about. An indirect report, while safer, could still be traced to you.

There are no easy answers for this problem. The only rules are to proceed with caution until you understand the situation more fully. Also, recognize that even if you do understand the problem, you can't always create a favorable outcome. Your best protection is to form a "network" of friends and colleagues. Here, if the worst happened, you'd use the network to help you move to another position.

Finally, let's discuss the most common *personal* breakpoint you'll face as a trainee. It's called First-Job Blues, and it happens more often than you'd think.

Breakpoint Signals

You're tired, depressed, lonely. After spending the summer on the job, you go back to your college homecoming in the fall and you feel a painful rush of nostalgia. You yearn to relive your college career. How much better you'd do now! You duck your friends' questions about how work is going. They seem so confident in their new jobs! You, on the other hand, dread the very thought of returning to work. Worse, you're convinced your dread is a sure sign of impending failure.

The problem? You may have the First-Job Blues.

Breakpoint Forces

In a nutshell, by changing cultures, you've put yourself in career shock. You're not at the top of the heap anymore. You're no longer a senior; you're not even a freshman who will inevitably become a senior in just four years. The road to the "top" is murky and ill-defined. You probably don't really know where the "top" is, unless you have an unusually clear picture of your career path.

Meanwhile, you know you're on the bottom now. Or if you don't, people with more seniority will soon make that point crystal clear. They've suffered the same indignities before you, and it's human nature for them to want to "get a bit of their own back."

Other shocks:

1. You've been part of the college or grad school world, where the product is you. How well you advance, score, and place in your class upon graduation is the major concern of your former "company"— i.e., your school. The rules have changed. Now you're a small part of a company whose major concern is a different product. You no

longer hold center stage. What's more, your bosses' major concerns have little to do with your career or even advancement. Your college faculty was paid to teach, evaluate, and help you advance. But now, your superiors are more concerned with advancing themselves, their products, and the company, often in that order.

2. You've been trained to think in far grander and broader terms than your initial work will require. Your opinions on matters that are properly the concerns of top management will be encouraged rarely, if at all, and will probably be resented or stifled if you persist.

Breakpoint Strategy

How to cope with the First-Job Blues? Do not give in to self-pity and petulance when you're on the job, no matter what anyone says about "letting it all hang out" or showing your "true feelings." Away from work, you might commiserate with friends you can trust, but keep it light. Crying doesn't help. Try to laugh about the indignities that go with being a "rookie." You got through fraternity/sorority initiation, didn't you? How about the freshman year away from home?

Best cure? Turn the situation around. Be a "support person" to other trainees in your training group. The effort will get you out of your shell, and besides making some good and perhaps valuable friendships, you'll reap the added benefits of strengthening a network of contacts that can last throughout your career.

Added Bonus: Supporting your fellow trainees may also score points with the company evaluators, who look to see how you relate to your peer group when evaluating executive potential. A West Point study, in fact, found that peer-group opinion was the most important predictor of future career advancement.

Bottom Line: Take heart. You won't be a trainee forever.

Other Breakpoint Strategies

1. *Keep tabs on other trainees in your group.* This is your class. When the others move, you move. If there's a fixed time, you'll know when it's time to move. If the time is flexible, keep your ear to the ground. When you hear that your classmate Stan Smith got a full depart-

ment to manage, this could mean the decision on you is imminent. Now's the time to go to your boss and lay out where you want to move. Don't be shy or withdrawn. If done tactfully, it never hurts to be direct.

2. *Keep your sights on the bottom line—i.e., don't think like a trainee.* Even though your opinion on "big picture" issues isn't welcomed most of the time, be ready for the rare occasion. Certainly think about the larger issues. Don't let temporary "pecking order" pressures corrupt your viewpoint if you're certain you're right.

3. *Finally, keep your sights on "your" bottom line, your career chart.* When the company says "yes," make sure your own "yes" response is in accord with your long-range goals. If not, prepare your exit.

Checklist for Spouses

A. Dress. You may be used to seeing your spouse in the jeans and sweatshirt he/she wore in college. This new image is a change, and signals a "growing up" that may be hard to take. But don't knock it. Knocking it may cause a greater problem. If you're sarcastic or say the budget just doesn't allow for new clothes, you'll add tension to a career phase that's already filled with tension. You're no longer sharing college life. But don't allow this to cause you to put down his/her job. It might help if you see old friends who are going through the same experiences.

B. Help your spouse see the big picture—the long-term view of his/her career—while mastering the short-term. You know what your spouse really wants. Help keep things on track.

C. If you both work, it's likely that you and your spouse will be in the trainee phase simultaneously. If you are, be clear from the start about how to handle decisions like corporate relocations. When a factor, agree beforehand what's to be done and how you'll handle it. Some companies are willing to help the spouse relocate. Others promise help, but then don't come through. How will your spouse feel if he/she is forced to give up his/her job? Can you both take a short- or long-term commuter marriage? All your cards should be on the table before problems arise, so you won't be devastated when decision points are faced—and they doubtless will be. Several years ago it was taken for granted that when the husband was transferred the wife and family went along. With more women in executive and professional ranks, the picture is changing. A recent survey we undertook shows that, increasingly, husbands are following wives when relocations are necessary. One case comes to mind where the wife was a patent attorney with expertise in the medical field and her husband was a computer expert. When a job opportunity in her company became available there was no question. The family took the new job on the Coast and the husband quickly found work with another company. His computer skills were far more transferable to a broader group than was her highly technical specialized experience.

D. Marital tensions may be especially great if you are in the trainee phase together. It's especially important to take care of your relationship—don't let company tensions erode your marriage.

When company socializing, remember what a help or hindrance you can be. Try to take a personal interest in the people he or she brings home, even if it's not the boss you're talking to. This could be the start of your spouse's "network," a friendship that will pay big dividends later on—to both of you.

Chapter 8

Initial Responsibility
The Young Turk

Capsule Summary

Your first step beyond the trainee phase rarely takes you to the corridors of power. Odds are you'll have more than enough responsibility to earn your keep, but you'll get the unglamorous, painstaking chores that your superiors want to avoid and usually delegate downward. Expect plenty of encouragement to develop performance skills to boost your productivity. Your boss may want each task done yesterday, and may remind you frequently that he could "knock this thing off in five minutes."

But productivity alone is rarely enough to move you out of this stage to a managerial level. Key points to remember:

Your primary performance virtues are dependability and integrity. You run interference. Your boss calls the signals, carries the ball, and scores the touchdowns.

To move up, you'll need to show leadership potential. The ways to do this at your present level have little to do with giving orders, and much to do with anticipating what will be needed without being told.

You must choose the right assignments, department, and boss. A "family" or "team" atmosphere at work may be pleasant, but it can distract you from your real career goals and chew up valuable years.

Observe your competition—both at your company and elsewhere—keep an eye out for signs of present peril or new opportunity.

Performance Breakpoints

The thrill quickly faded after Mary Williams received her first promotion to manager of three telephone company offices. "The training program emphasized leadership," she recalled woefully. "Big-picture stuff, company policy, all that. But in reality, the line supervisors under me did all the interpersonal work, and my boss, the district manager, made all the decisions. I was supposed to be in charge, but no one thought I had any real authority. It's the union and the seniority system that really run things. All I did was write reports and memos that I could have turned out my freshman year. I couldn't wait to get promoted."

Alas, Mary didn't get promoted. Asked to stop by the personnel director's office one Friday afternoon, she was dazed to learn she was being given a new assignment at the same level as the one she'd held for two years. Worse, from Mary's viewpoint, the new position was with the division's research staff, rather than in operations. "We feel you need a bit more time to master the fundamentals" was the only reason she got for the decision.

Mary came to us convinced she'd been done in by politics, sexism, and a personality conflict. "I knew more than my boss did," she claimed. "Sure, there was a lot of technical nonsense that I didn't bother with— why should I? That's for the operators to know, not me. I'll never use that stuff. The only reason my boss harped on it was to cover up. I had better ideas than he did and he knew it. Work became a constant battle, with him trying to put me in my place. Some days I didn't even want to get out of bed, I felt so worn out."

After she had vented her frustration and reflected further, however, Mary recalled a few events that might have given the company's decision some justification. At several meetings, her boss had had to delay the discussion while Mary looked up some key points of that "technical nonsense." One report had been returned from the VP's office because procedural details hadn't been followed. Another time, her boss had been embarrassed by his superior because he didn't know some key statistics about Mary's offices—statistics Mary didn't know either.

"I guess that's what they were paying me for," Mary finally admitted.

Breakpoint Signals

Jealousy, resentment, and fatigue are common signals of what we call the "subordinate syndrome."

Breakpoint Forces

No one likes drudgery, and no one wants to be treated like a trainee, especially after moving through the trainee level. Mary's boss, like most others, had taken a positive approach to loading her with unpalatable chores, chores he did not wish to perform. He then asserted his authority by belittling the tasks he assigned her. "This is a piece of cake," he'd say as he dropped yet another thick sheaf of telephone-usage reports on her desk. Frequently he'd boast that he could "knock this kind of thing off in no time" if he'd wanted to.

Jealousy and resentment were natural responses on Mary's part. But these responses didn't help her and ultimately lost her a promotion.

Mary also responded with fatigue. At first, she thought she was simply worn out by the "personality conflict" and trying to hold her own against her boss's domineering tactics. After some reflection, however, she discovered a paradox. The less grindstone-style "homework" she did, the more fatigued she became.

Why? Because Mary had to cover up for her lack of preparation, the strain of "faking it" was worse than the strain of grinding out the work. When a burdensome task is mastered, there's a sense of uplift, of achievement, and a real lightening of the work load. Also, since doing the work makes you more efficient, your future tasks become easier.

"I *was* faking it," Mary finally said. "I wanted to move up so much I tried to pretend I was already promoted. That's what really wore me out."

Point to Remember: Everyone wants to move up before they've had time to learn the job fully. Daily media hype of fast-track managers on the way up can intensify natural ambition. Personnel policies that reserve top assignments for early achievers add fuel to the flames. Don't let these forces cause you to lose sight of your real goal: to master the job. If you accomplish this earlier than your colleagues, so much the better.

The forces that cause "subordinate syndrome" in the first place are rooted in the past. The boss paid dues during the early years, grinding out interference for his/her boss. Now it's the boss's turn to score the touch-downs and get the glory. Your job is to take the lumps running interference.

Fair enough? It will seem more equitable when you're in your boss's position.

Breakpoint Strategy 1

Couldn't be simpler. DO YOUR HOMEWORK. But you're not a trainee anymore, and nobody wants to teach you, so you've got to train yourself. This means testing yourself, motivating yourself, and rewarding yourself. Become your own instructor, and give first priority to learning what will make your boss look good.

Breakpoint Strategy 2

Don't waste time reinventing the wheel. Ask yourself, "How did they do this last year?" We know this rule flies in the face of all the clichés about creativity, originality, and fresh new thinking. But it works, and it's necessary. You can dream up all the new procedures you want, but don't act on them until you've learned what you're trying to change. Learn the "company way" as well as the "right way." Your department and your company both need to appear consistent and coordinated. They've been around more than the few months you've been there, and the odds are great that someone has faced and solved your problem before. Build on that effort and research, plunder the files. If your file search turns up a hopeless muddle, *then* make a fresh start.

Breakpoint Strategy 3

Formal training. Don't jump into degree programs or night courses until you know they're necessary to help you on your career path. Going back to school may be necessary, but unless you're with a company where cross-training is overtly encouraged, it puts you at a real disadvantage. You may be perceived as a student. Worse, your commitment at the office is perceived as being part-time or diluted. Take a full-time formal course of study only where it is required, or encouraged, or if you're planning to leave the company. Otherwise your best solution is night classes, correspondence courses, and cassettes. A rule with this kind of training is the same as that found in the trainee stage: *Make it look easy.*

Other Performance Breakpoints

I. "First Time Out"

For her second job out of law school, Joanne was hired by a small firm that put together multimillion-dollar equipment-leasing syndications, raising capital and providing tax shelter for their investors. Her duties during the first few months were primarily paperwork, preparing legal materials that would meet securities-law standards.

Then a "deal" came along, and a deadline for raising the investment funds loomed large just at the time the general counsel became ill. Joanne was sent with the firm's projections and write-up of the offering to the Big Eight accounting firm they used as outside consultants. Her job: to explain the deal with the numbers and show how the projections and tax losses were valid. The Big Eight accounting firm would then make its own analysis and write the opinion letter that would give security to potential investors. A simple task, she thought.

But her initial presentation was interrupted by one of the accounting firm's junior partners. A new facet of the tax law seemed to apply to her firm's deal—one that would require extensive analysis and research. In other words, there would most likely be a delay in the opinion-letter timetable and a hefty increase in the fee to the accountants.

Joanne was familiar with the tax law the accountants were discussing, but she hadn't been aware of the recent regulation that made it applicable to her firm's new deal. She asked for the copy of the regulations and the tax code, and after a quick review of both together with the junior partner accountant—who'd just written an article on the subject for an accounting journal—she was convinced that the accounting firm was correct.

So she phoned the office and got her two bosses—the president and vice-president of the firm—to tell them of the delay. Sensing that there'd be resistance, she placed the call using a speaker phone in the accounting firm's office with the junior partner present to deliver the news himself.

Predictably, there were howls of outrage when her bosses learned that the offering date would be set back by at least a week. Both bosses argued the point. One got a copy of the tax code and regulations and read it aloud over the phone, challenging the accounting firm's interpretation. The law couldn't apply, he said. It was completely illogical and the government would lose money.

The accounting firm's junior partner held his own in the debate for a time, but the two bosses weren't prepared to give in. Their arguments began to verge on the irrational. At this point Joanne joined the debate— but made the grave error of taking the side of the accounting firm. As soon as they realized which side she was arguing for, her bosses became even more incensed. She was brusquely ordered to leave the materials with the accounting firm and return to the office.

Thereafter she noted a distinct chill. "From that day on, things were never the same," she recalls. "The executive vice-president especially—it seemed as if he couldn't wait to get rid of me after that one day. I wish I'd known enough to keep my mouth shut."

The firm did let Joanne go within three months of the incident. Unfair? Probably. In fact, almost certainly. But had Joanne been more careful, the incident need not have happened.

Breakpoint Forces

Most companies operate on an "us versus others" emotional level. Rationality to the contrary, emotions of loyalty transcend professionalism for many if not most company executives. Whether this trait is positive or negative isn't at issue here; we're only pointing out the trait so you can identify and be sensitive to it.

Breakpoint Strategy

When you're outside the company, always remember who's paying your salary. If you become involved in the kind of situation Joanne found herself in, never join a debate on the side of the opposition against your boss. Few bosses will forgive a subordinate for making them lose face in front of an outsider. "Had I known, I'd have come straight back to the office and relayed the accounting firm's position," Joanne says now. "Then I could have had time to think about other alternatives, like using a different accounting firm. What really galls me now is that history proved the accountants wrong and my former boss right—even though the other position looked so attractive at the time."

II. You Get Stuck with a "Tar Baby."

At twenty-five, Eddie Grant thought he'd taken a great leap forward when selected for promotion to market development manager at nearly twice his initial salary. But he soon discovered that his boss, the marketing manager, had grossly inflated sales projections for his group. Eddie protested. There was no way he or anyone else could meet these goals!

Certain that he had to make a stand to protect himself, he confronted his boss directly. The boss reacted with a campaign to fire Eddie for not working up to potential and lack of enthusiasm about the product.

Outcome? The boss was wrong, and this point was noted by top management. So the boss got "moved laterally." Eddie didn't fare well, either, however. He wasn't fired, but he was promoted to marketing manager for a low-priority product. In relative obscurity, he soon found his career at a standstill.

Breakpoint Signals

You're drawn into a confrontation with your boss.

Breakpoint Forces

No company functions with insubordination. Whether you're right or wrong, a fight with your boss is like punching a tar baby. The conflict is seldom resolved quickly or cleanly, and most often is resolved against you. Many young managers like Eddie do get fired by bosses who need to cover up their own mistakes—and who often succeed at the cover-up. Not every boss who inflates projections gets caught. This "fast and dirty" method of impressing superiors may work well, especially if the boss is a rising star who'll be moved elsewhere before the impossible results must be achieved.

Breakpoint Strategy

Avoid confrontation. Look to history to verify if the goals your boss sets for you are achievable or not. If you discover there's no way you can measure up to the projections, discreetly activate your job-seeking campaign, either inside the company or outside. Try to have a new position available well before the day of reckoning. In the meantime, don't oppose your boss's impossible demands. Instead, simply refrain from comment whenever the subject is raised. The silence may become deafening.

The same rationale holds for confrontation with those on your level, your peers.

Breakpoint Signals

Someone isn't producing, and it's affecting your ability to produce.

Breakpoint Forces

You'd like the luxury of saying, "That's not my job." You want to believe that the company system works. You want to be able to blame the party who's letting down their side. You don't want to, nor should you, do that person's job. All this is true enough. But—getting to the two-yard line doesn't put points on the scoreboard. You're not adding to your career laurels if you're known as the person who did a fine job on your department's most recent failure.

Breakpoint Strategy

Get the job done. Do whatever is necessary, even when it includes the work of others. Find a way to *indirectly* let more than one person know what you're doing—without complaining. Ideal: two above you, two below you. The system will work when people learn who's producing and who isn't.

Remember, it's possible that the performance or productivity goals your boss sets are legitimate, so don't take these plans as a face-value summary of everything you need to do to succeed. Try to determine the criteria you're not told about. The best way to determine the unstated criteria is to observe who got promoted and what they did right in management's eyes. Get your own set of criteria together. Then have a chat with your boss. "Here's what I've been thinking I should emphasize. Am I on target?"

PERSONAL BREAKPOINTS: "YOUNG TURK SYNDROME"

Breakpoint Signals

You're increasingly irritated with the system. Each day you see more flaws, more inefficiencies, more need for catering to the whims and petty egos of those above you. You daydream constantly about making a break to a better-organized company where you can maximize your talents—or maybe even start up on your own.

Breakpoint Forces

Sure, the old duffers could use some shaking up. But nobody's perfect. The real problem is what your initial taste of responsibility is doing to some long-suppressed resentments. Unless you're working for a very unusual organization, there's a pecking order where you work, and you're still a "peckee." You're irked by all the irritating, sometimes superficial hoops you're required to jump through.

Breakpoint Strategy

To counter frustrations that go with your relatively powerless position, begin to focus on building independence. We don't mean daydreaming about leading commando raids or political rallies. Nor do we mean cultivating oddball dress styles or other personal quirks. This is not the attention you want.

A number of years ago there was an advertising agency on the West Coast named Honig, Cooper and Harrington. It has since been merged with another agency, but at the time it was an up-and-coming organization. We had done some search work for the agency which resulted in the hiring of an account supervisor on a major piece of the business—as I recall, a part of the Clorox account. The exec we put with the company began riding a motorcycle to work, and a few days later I received a call from Bill Honig, the president, looking for reassurance that he had hired a responsible person to manage the account and relate to the Clorox management.

What to do? First try to accommodate the system by taking inventory of the things you do have control over, the things no one can take away from you. First, set time during the workday you can reserve for yourself, quiet time—and fill it with activity that will pay you dividends later on. During these hours you can work on your own training program, on your top-priority project, or on any of the other work-related activities you've postponed to keep up with your boss's demands. (These pages contain a few suggestions.) The important thing is that *you've* chosen the activity and that you *know* you'll benefit directly from what you're doing. This knowledge puts you in control; you're working for yourself.

Second, develop the habit of reviewing your day's activity with the question "What was in it for me?" Identify things you learned or contacts you made that will later benefit you, whether or not you stay with the same company. Keep a record of these events and periodically review the record to see what you can build on.

Third, invest 10 percent of your paycheck. James Clavell, author of *Noble House*, called it your "go-to-hell money," because if you have enough of it, that's what you can tell people. The amount you set aside will not give you this capability, at least at first. But the psychological effect will create some security and be comforting.

The *reverse* of the "Young Turk syndrome" we call "blue skies, no candy."

Breakpoint Signals

You find yourself thinking how meaningful your work is, how dedicated the others in the office are, and what a wonderful human being your boss is. But your pay falls far below your expectations. "This isn't a business to be in if you want to get rich," people say when the subject comes up. Sometimes their voices are tinged with pride, as if to imply that they're working for values more lofty than others.

Breakpoint Forces

Friendliness, warmth, and mutual respect from co-workers and your boss are very powerful persuaders, especially when you're young and eager for the respect of your elders. The pleasure of working under these conditions fits your college ideals of dedication and inner fulfillment. The "team" intoxication may be wonderful. But it also may blind you to some of your other needs. Remember, pay is equated by others with your success. If you wake up and try to make a change, you'll find your age/salary-level formula doesn't take you where you want to go next.

In the mid-1970s I had a conversation with a senior-level executive who had a prominent name and heritage. He was very concerned about an offer he was evaluating from the Continental Can Company in New York. He felt that the company had, while offering him an excellent job to run a major division, scrimped on the salary package.

I suggested that he approach the top management to find out why. Sure enough, the response was that with a name found on products sold across America he certainly did not need the money.

Yes, his experience met all the criteria, but did it make sense to be penalized because he was fortunate enough to have accumulated some wealth? He turned the offer down.

Remember, when you're looking for a job, those evaluating you will form judgments from many pieces of data. One key piece will be how much money your current employer feels you're worth.

Breakpoint Strategy

Get out your career chart. What do you want five years from now? Look around you at work, at those who've been around five years longer than you. How many are where you want to be? This exercise is likely to show that something's got to change. Either change your career-chart goals (assuming that you really have changed your values) or plan to leave.

Point to Ponder: What you view as idealism may simply be an ego response to being properly stroked by the boss and the "team" at work. Recognizing a "blue skies, no candy" syndrome in others is relatively easy. You'll need a lot of willpower to spot the syndrome in yourself.

POLITICAL BREAKPOINTS

Capsule Summary

Politics can be a major factor in every career phase, but at the time of initial responsibility it's especially important. Expect to be called a "Young Turk" (after the political group who overthrew the Ottoman establishment just before World War I). The phrase indicates you've got the right stuff—the drive to get ahead. With bastions of established executives to keep the new generation in place, people know you've got to overcome other egos to get anywhere. But at this stage, you have little real power. If you attack like a revolutionary, you'll make enemies and lose ground.

Your best political bet—and most important political task at this stage of your career—is to form a strong alliance with a strong boss and get some victories on the scoreboard.

The Right Boss. How do you know if you've got the right boss? More important, if you don't have the right boss, what can you do about it?

Breakpoint Signals: The Hot Seat

At U.S. Steel Corporation, Laura's boss had a reputation for brilliance —and for chewing up young assistants. Once a mill foreman, he'd come up through the ranks to division manager, in charge of operations at more than a dozen mills throughout the Northeast. From his assistants he demanded reports and more reports—more than any of them could cope with. Worse, he called each assistant to his office for degrading half-hour "review" sessions, during which he nitpicked as many of these reports as time would allow. There was occasional praise, but only frequently enough, it seemed, to keep the unfortunate assistant off balance.

After her first exhausting month trying to follow his commands, Laura changed strategy in two ways. First, while he was away she analyzed his past and future appointments calendars, comparing them with his incoming correspondence from the company vice-president. She applied the results to her own work load to create her own "hot item" list for each week. During the following weeks, Laura put each "hot item" on her boss's desk before he asked for it. Where this took time away from other items, she added a "weekly update" page instead.

Laura's second strategy was more subtle and took more time. Noticing that her boss hadn't used his share of the division's redecorating budget since he'd taken over three years before, she waited till a week after a visit from the vice-president to whom her boss reported. Then she presented her boss with glossy brochure photos of several office layout plans, and hinted that a talk with the VP's administrative assistant had given her the distinct impression that the VP wanted her boss to set a better corporate example by projecting an up-to-the-times image. In the same vein, she arranged with personnel to replace the boss's long-suffering personal secretary with another whose temperament was more maternal.

The result? The boss's crotchety manners didn't change, but the work Laura was assigned changed radically. Rather than simply compiling data, Laura was soon evaluating some of it and working with the district-level people to improve their results. Her job, in short, changed from being purely a staff assistant to an executive. Within a year she was given her own district office to manage.

Breakpoint Signals

The boss seems unreasonably unhappy with or unsure about what you're doing.

Breakpoint Forces

Each boss is preoccupied with his or her own problems, not with yours. Since you, however, are an easy target, you may become the lightning rod for frustrations.

This problem is compounded by a fast-track system, which frequently puts rising-star supervisors in positions they haven't yet learned. Laura's boss, for example, was accustomed to supervising people on the assembly line. He still felt defensive toward others who had not worked in the plant, and reacted by making a compulsion out of the technique that had proved successful for him in the mill: attention to detail. Not only are bosses like Laura's unequipped with technical expertise to train their subordinates; they lack managerial ability to train their subordinates and motivate them constructively. The result can be bruised egos and frustration.

Breakpoint Strategy: Your Boss's Career Chart

You won't get anywhere pointing out your boss's managerial shortcomings or insecurities by direct confrontation. Instead, create a career chart for your boss. Determine where he or she is on the chart and then analyze the needs. If your boss has been in a supervisory position a short while, don't expect much instruction or help. Also, don't expect to find evidence of managerial skills that come with years of experience. You'll have to toughen your own hide to compensate for clumsiness at instruction or motivation.

If you can learn background detail about your boss, incorporate it into your analysis of "boss" needs. Laura used this technique, relating her boss's prior blue-collar experience to his present insecurity at the managerial level. She compensated for that with office decor changes that would boost his ego and personnel changes that would make him feel more comfortable.

There may be nothing you can do to change your boss's habits or mannerisms, but by identifying needs you can tailor your performance for maximum worth and get maximum benefit from whatever recommendations may be given.

Creating a career chart for your boss will also show you his or her breakpoints, whether your boss is aware of them or not. For example, if your boss has a fast-track goal for a top-level position, and you're at a company where your boss's area of expertise is not critical to the company's success, you know you may soon have a new boss. The same is true if your boss's expertise *is* critical (or soon will be) and he or she is a steady-path person. In these cases, you'll need to take into account your boss's need to become known outside the company so that he or she can successfully change jobs.

Key. Recognizing that your boss is at a breakpoint may be just as important as recognizing your own breakpoints.

Finding Another Boss. And what if you determine that your boss *won't* benefit your career? Suppose you see your boss as either at a dead end or not long for the job. The recommendation you're working for will carry little or no weight.

Breakpoint Signals

When you've created your boss's career chart, the signals will be easier to read. Make a point to notice how superiors treat your boss. How often do they write, phone, or come to visit? How much weight do they give the boss's opinions at meetings? What's their general manner when they're on-site? What is the budget for your department and when was it last increased and by how much? How do your department's results compare with those of others?

Warning: Discretion is the watchword here. No boss wants to let subordinates in on information that reflects on his or her own performance. But keep your eyes open and use what you see, or what you already know, to make a hard-headed appraisal of your boss's prospects and potential. Don't be misled by your hope that doing a good job for this one person is all you need to accomplish. You may come to work Monday to find that your boss has been fired.

The best way to get a new boss, of course, is to be promoted. If that seems unlikely in view of your present boss's prospects, your task is to attract favorable attention within your company. At the same time, activate your job-seeking connections on the outside.

Several years ago I met a very bright young woman with the Bristol-Myers Company. She complained that she felt dead-ended because her boss was never going to be promoted. She was correct in her assessment, and after accepting the painful truth, planned her move. Her search outside Bristol-Myers turned up several nice opportunities and she wound up with a fine company in a job two levels above the one at Bristol-Myers.

Within the company, you must polish your image. As superficial as it sounds, you have few other ways to favorably impress those who may not have time to give your performance an evaluation on its merits. Since many managers put off personnel reviews and performance evaluations, you may have to push a bit.

Many managers take a position either that they don't have the time or that they are more interested in the future. In reality, they're doing you a disservice and often use these excuses to avoid giving employees the constructive or negative feedback they need. One of the most stressful tasks for a manager is communicating negative feedback.

Key your calendar to dates when superiors will be calling or visiting. Make it a point to have whatever information they're likely to want at your fingertips and don't hesitate to ask for their feedback. Try to avoid the mistake of "dressing up" for the occasion. Your appearance should convey the same message as your performance: that you're *consistently* on top of things. Your desk and surroundings should create the same impression.

Does it work? There are no guarantees. But you can bet that a messy desk, unkempt dress, and uncertain manner when asked for data won't be of benefit.

Strengthening the Alliance: "On the Carpet". Barry, the young and only accountant for a small but highly successful brokerage firm, turned pale when the firm's general counsel showed him the notice from the state banking commission. What happened? Barry had paid that year's registration fee at the end of the month, with the rest of the bills, overlooking the computer print that said "must be received by the 21st." It didn't matter that the invoice had come in on the 8th, and that the firm, as a policy, always paid late to maximize "float." Some gleeful state bureaucrat had enforced the deadline and revoked the firm's license.

Barry thought he was finished. He'd been overworked, and the president of the firm had been riding him hard. This mistake could be the last straw. The firm was legally dead until its license could be reinstated. The entire application process—dozens of pages of forms and photographs—would have to be refiled before the firm could sell anything to anyone within the state. And the president would have to sign the forms. There was no way to keep him from finding out what had happened. Barry's one hope was a plan he'd worked out with the firm's counsel.

That afternoon Barry drove two hours to the state capital, picked up the forms, and spent a few minutes with the state officer in charge of processing the application. That night, with a little help from the firm's counsel, Barry sat at a typewriter with the previous year's forms and filled out the new forms. The next morning he was in the office of the firm's president with the completed forms, each one tagged for signature.

"The state bounced our renewal because I was late with the fee," Barry explained. "Here's what we have to file today." The president froze. His eyes went cold. Then after a long moment, he reached for the pen. "You just got fired and rehired," he said.

Breakpoint Signal

You know you've made a major blunder.

Breakpoint Forces

Everyone makes mistakes. Bosses make their share, and most expect their subordinates to err, though they may not admit it. The major consideration from your boss's viewpoint is what he'll have to do to correct the mistake. If you've already minimized the corrective effort your boss will have to make, you are 90 percent of the way to having undone your misdeed.

Breakpoint Strategy

Are you certain how to correct the mistake? Carefully analyze the problem, then start toward a solution before your boss learns what's happening. This, of course, assumes that your efforts will not make matters worse, so you have nothing to lose by taking action. It may not work, but inaction could lead to months of "what if" wondering after you've been fired.

SPECIAL POINTERS

Breakpoint Signal

You get your first nice office: a non-steel-case desk, a credenza, a view, side chairs, maybe even a carpet. Should you decorate?

Breakpoint Forces

The answer is "no"—even if your firm gives employees a free hand. Sure, you should move in family pictures (to the credenza, not your desk) and your diplomas, and flowers if you like them. But beyond these obvious signals that this turf is now yours, keep it spartan. If you install curtains, a coffeepot, knickknack shelves, and the like, you may communicate that you're really settling in—a gesture that can be interpreted not as loyalty but rather as lack of ambition, or worse. Superiors may be quick to cast you as a homebody who can be taken for granted, or as someone who's reached the top goal in life.

Breakpoint Strategy

Avoid "Hang in there, baby" posters that show a cute little kitten clinging to a chinning bar, plaques with self-deprecating slogans (e.g., "Today is the worst day of the rest of my life"), newspaper and magazine cartoons depicting harried secretaries and overbearing bosses. People may see you as struggling to stay afloat, and the fact that you seem to be taking it all with a grin won't help you.

The best image? A clean desk. Look as if your job's "in your hip pocket" so you'll give the impression of being ready to move up. You'll get better treatment—people will respect your implied expertise and "together" image. Since you appear to have what it takes to move to greener pastures, they'll want to keep you. Added bonus: A clean desk *will* make you more efficient, since you'll concentrate on the task at hand without letting other work distract you. Hint: This is one goal you can achieve painlessly and instantly. Just move your in basket, out basket, and all work-in-process materials to a separate worktable or credenza.

A CHANCE TO CHANGE CAREER FIELDS

Sooner or later you'll probably be faced with this prospect. It has special problems and opportunities when you're at this stage. Now's the time to change career fields, if you're unattached and can avoid the strain of taking a family back to square one with you. If you're undecided about switching fields, the decision to make the shift should be postponed until you've had the chance to savor a few benefits from your present work and weigh the possibilities. Often discontent with your boss or rank will surface as a wish to try another field. Imagine yourself in those greener pastures, but with the same boss and the same hierarchy. That's what you're likely to find. Avoid wasting more years of training to arrive at a similar position of discontent.

Women should be especially cautious about changing fields. Reason? In this less than ideal work world, women are especially vulnerable to being assigned menial tasks when they return to square one. Male bosses often ignore years of experience in a prior field—something they're less likely to do with a man. The result: In a career change, a woman may lose more time than a man. Thus the sacrifice can be proportionately greater.

The first checkpoint for evaluating career change, of course, is your career chart and the asset inventory analysis of your abilities.

Changing Locations. This is another matter. A move to another country may be good, particularly if you're to be an assistant to a high-level person. If your new post would be relatively obscure, it's best to pass it up —out of sight, out of mind. Find out first if you've been sought out, or if someone simply wants to see you out of the country and, perhaps, out of the competition.

The Colgate Palmolive Company has for years maintained that since so much of its business is international, an executive must have international experience before being considered for a senior-level general management promotion in the United States.

While the positive effect on the corporate management structure is obvious, two negatives are present which, probably more than any other reason, cause executives to leave Colgate.

First, in spite of uprooting the family and making the sacrifice to move overseas, there is no corporate commitment about either the nature of the assignment or what job you'll be brought into Stateside when your time overseas is up. Over the years, people having made the commitment for the company have occasionally found "no suitable job" when they returned. While this happens infrequently, the stories are exaggerated and passed around until a regular occurrence of this scenario seems the rule rather than the exception.

Second, and most important from a career development standpoint, the United States is without doubt the world business leader. When a high-powered executive takes an assignment in South America, for instance, there is often a sudden realization that the country he has been assigned to is twenty or perhaps as much as thirty years behind the United States. This is not a problem; trace the past twenty to thirty years in the United States, find out what worked, and play it again, right? Very well, what happens when after five years or so you return to the States? Your competition has pulled ahead by at least five years while you've been playing old records.

Stay current. Try to avoid becoming customized for any company too early in your career or without a well-designed loop back home.

On the other hand, take a look around at those in the organization who are in positions you might aspire to. How many of them served abroad? At what stage of their careers? In what positions? If the geographic spot you're offered has led to success for them, it may do the same for you.

Checklist for Spouses

1. The greatest career problem couples today are likely to face at this stage comes from going through it together. If both husband and wife are working, it's highly probable they'll enter the work force together and wind up in the throes of Young Turkdom at the same time. Which means that all the frustrations, anxieties, etc., that are bottled up at work may surface at home.

   One couple we know had to make a deal not to talk about work at home. Another couple made it a point to go jogging together when they got home—releasing tensions and getting the workday "off their chests" at the same time. Going through the young Turk phase at the same time can also mean that you may not get to spend as much time as you'd like together. You may be working late, trying to make the big jump onto the fast track, and it may seem there just are not enough hours in the day for your marriage. Make time.

2. Changing location is a problem you'll face through most of your careers. One young couple we know joined a major corporation together. A few years later the husband felt it was time to move on. And out of the company. The couple interviewed together and found jobs together in another major city—though this time not at the same company. Everything sounds as if the couple made all the right moves and should live happily ever after. But for the wife, the move was difficult even though it was 100 percent right for her career. An extraordinary musician as well as a doctor of computer science, she'd been part of a women's singing group and the alto in a quartet for several years. And recently she'd been acting director of the larger group. The move meant letting go of an avocation. If she had refused to go, her husband would have understood. But they kept their eyes on the big picture, and in the long run it will pay off.

Strategy: Talk out the issue ahead of time. Know in advance if your spouse is willing to move:

—to another place in the United States (how far away and if there's anyplace he or she wouldn't move to on a bet);

—to another country (and for how long—and what about the kids and schools?);

—at all—your spouse may be on the fast track at his/her company, may love it, and may think a move an unreasonable request. Or he/she may simply be happy with life where you live now. Knowing ahead of time, though, will give you a clearer picture of your options. You'll be likely to try to change your spouse's mind if a terrific opportunity comes up, of course, and the process will be easier since you've come this far.

The results of one of our recent surveys indicate that lifestyle has risen in importance to the top of the list for younger managers. A number of years ago young couples were far more prone to accept jobs in less desirable locations to get ahead. Today, along with a "working to live the way we'd like" attitude comes the "weekend break to do what we want." Camping in the mountains is tough in Iowa.

3. If your wife is returning to the work force after the interruption of raising a family, problems and frustrations she encounters as she gets back on track will probably be amplified by the age factor. Bosses are likely to be younger than she. Secretarial chores and "gofer" tasks may be more demeaning. Husbands can be particularly supportive here—especially if they're willing to help with a "here's how I did it —you can too" attitude.

4. Non-employed spouses should remember that though the employed member may be spending what seems like an inordinate amount of time working, this isn't (at least not necessarily) to avoid being at home. Your spouse is building a future for you both and won't be encouraged by complaints about keeping late hours or occasionally having to work on weekends. Balance is key here. Hard work sprinkled with recreation.

5. Ask your spouse about *your* career. Where does he or she expect you to be in five years? Your mate's answer may surprise you, and you may find it puts the pressure on. For instance, he or she may see you as a fast-track type when what you really want is a safe, quiet, middle-level management position. On the other hand, it may relieve some needless pressure to perform and move up.

6. Don't let your love for your spouse keep you from speaking the truth. If your mate comes home with complaints and you can think of ways to improve, lay it on the line. Tactfully, of course. Mary Williams's husband—a manager himself—had been aware for a long time that she just wasn't up on the details as much as she should have been. He couldn't think of a way to tell her without hurting her feelings— even though he deals with similar problems every day of the week at work. It may be more difficult with your spouse, but kinder in the long run. You can help by taking a positive interest in detail that your spouse finds demeaning or boring, but don't try to fake it. You'll only compound the cynicism. Instead, focus on rewarding your spouse when results have been achieved, and on comforting a bruised ego resulting from clumsy guidance or criticism from a heavy-handed boss.

7. Odds are that you'll be pinched for money now. If your spouse wants to save, recognize that saving may give your spouse more confidence. On the other hand, emphasis on positive thinking at work may blind

your spouse to the family's financial needs. The "blue skies, no candy" syndrome is difficult for working spouses to recognize from the inside. If the non-working spouse goes out and gets a job, however, the message usually comes across loud and clear.

8. Much has been made of a person's ability to put a working spouse's career on the skids due to shortcomings in manners, social poise, breeding, wardrobe, and the like. It's all true. Tests of these traits probably won't impact greatly at this level, but eventually you will be evaluated. Now's the time to see where you want to be in five or ten years, and to ensure that you prepare yourself so that you don't get in the way of progress. If you think this warning advice sounds superficial, simplistic, and callous, you're right. But it matches the treatment you and your spouse will receive if you aren't prepared.

Chapter 9

Middle Management
Steady Path

Capsule Summary

When you're on the steady path, your main objective is to produce. Since you'll almost certainly be urged to get on the fast track if you're a success, there lies the danger.

Be sure to keep your goals clear and your priorities straight.

At this level, you may encounter problems with your immediate subordinates who "knew you when." Establishing the distance necessary to be "the boss" can pose problems, but with your peers you've got a political advantage in having chosen the steady path. However, some peers and superiors will view your choice as a weakness.

You'll have to show them you're a force to be reckoned with, even though you're not heading for the corner office.

PERFORMANCE BREAKPOINTS

When Netta Larsen's boss retired, she was the first woman to be promoted from a plant manager position to regional production manager. She was now in charge of three plants, each with its own production difficulties and union problems.

Her company gave her the same training it did all upper management. She had several weeks of theory courses in management-employee development, labor relations, and financial planning and was encouraged to look at the "big picture."

She promised herself that since she'd worked her way up through the ranks, she would keep her employees well motivated by developing their talents and providing opportunities for personal growth. After all, her training supervisor had told her during her first week's seminar at the home office that she was a living example of what could be accomplished if a line worker had the right attitude.

In the months that followed, Netta inaugurated many new and innovative programs. They ranged from after-hours discussions on production techniques to group training seminars, from cross-training on different work stations to group counseling regarding marital problems and the two-career marriage.

The employees loved it, but after the first two months productivity indexes dropped at all three plants. For the first time, Netta found herself with union problems. One office wanted a VCR to tape the Phil Donahue show every morning and play it back during the coffee break and lunch hour.

"Of course, that was a pre-union election gimmick," Netta recalls, "but it made me realize that I'd lost control of the situation. The girls were treating the job like a summer camp."

It took nearly a year to shift the focus back to productivity and to gracefully withdraw from the "personal development" Netta had begun with such good intentions. During that year, Netta's credibility with her bosses was in tatters. Her productivity index, it turned out, was the bottom line for them.

"All that other 'big picture,' material they threw at me in training went completely by the boards when they saw that profits were down," Netta recalls. "I did everything they said, and the end result was I lost at least two raises. It wasn't until I realized how the game was played that I got things under control. They really don't mean what they say."

Breakpoint Signals

When mid-level managers get too close to subordinates, frivolous union demands and frequent complaints about "alienation" and lack of "fulfillment" are symptoms of the difficulty. But the real signal is a lack of team spirit, or the absence of concern for productivity. Her plants' productivity indexes, of course, told Netta that she was out of sync with company needs.

Do not wait until your productivity index falls before you realize you've gotten your priorities mixed. Not only does this delay hurt the company, but it's also costly to you, either in promotions missed or in bonuses and raises foregone.

What to watch out for: Overemphasis on employee happiness in your directives to subordinates. The goals of the company do include employee satisfaction and good working conditions, of course, but these items are made possible only when the company is profitable.

Employee self-fulfillment in a loss-ridden company will be short-lived at best.

Breakpoint Forces

As corny as it seems, management will only be successful if people are committed to something beyond themselves. Without this commitment, you may build a collection of prima donnas, each with his or her mind on something other than the job.

Breakpoint Strategy

Playing autocrat won't give you the results you need, but you must establish a required distance so people take your goals for the company seriously.

Here's what you can do to help:

1. Eliminate discussion of your personal life in the office. You may have been friends with your subordinates in the past, asking for their advice. But today and from now on you need to show your employees that they should take your role at face value and not try to explain issues away by relating them to your personal life.

   Many a stern warning by a boss has been brushed aside by an overly familiar employee. It's easy to rationalize, "Well, he just had another fight with his wife this morning and he's taking it out on me."

2. Avoid a set routine. As you're evaluating people, don't let them become too secure in knowing what the "test" is going to be. This will prevent them from "faking it" and keep them alert.

3. Don't criticize one employee in front of another, and don't relate to

subordinates on an office-gossip level even though they may be close friends outside the office. Listen, but don't react.

4. When you praise someone either in private or in public, describe the act that you like and relate it to corporate goals. "This is the kind of productivity increase that will help us break into the southern market" is more effective than "Great job, Willie, atta boy!"

5. Take the opportunity to talk with employees out of the office, where your interest in their personal lives is more likely to be given the right interpretation. If you bring an employee into your office to just chat, you're saying in effect that work hours may be used for personal goals. But if you take time to chat away from the office—in the parking lot, in the lunchroom, off hours, etc.,—you're letting your employees know that they're important enough to learn about them on your *own* time, not company time. Remember, people at lower levels will emulate you. During business hours, keep the subject business: during non-business hours, non-business discussions. You're letting them know the proper time for personal discussions.

6. Don't always reveal the reasons behind your decisions. Close the door of your office from time to time when you are working alone and when you bring employees in for evaluation. Don't make the mistake of closing the door only when you're going to criticize an employee, or soon everyone will know exactly what the closed door means.

7. Never surprise an individual with criticism on a point that hasn't been covered previously. If you dislike personal telephone calls made on the job, for instance, say so publicly. Present your position as part of a speech on company or department goals or put them in a "general policy" memo to all, so that no one individual who is criticized can complain of being unfairly singled out.

8. The bottom line is still "us versus them." Set "harsh" decisions in the context of your company versus the competition. "No raises this quarter because the other side has cut prices and we've got to hold costs down." Or "Competition is laying off 15 percent of their staff, but we're going to try to keep everyone on board."

9. Use your background to provide examples for staff. If you've worked your way up through the ranks, you have a wonderful base from which you can encourage superior craft, a key to excellence. For instance, if you're managing a production facility, take time to praise the finer points of an employee's product. Point out subtleties only

an expert would notice. If you don't know the difference, ask one of your senior people in a private conference to go over the skills of the operation and determine what the three most difficult facets are.

PERSONAL BREAKPOINTS

Capsule Summary

The steady-path mid-level job has the great long-term advantage of stability.

But this advantage can also be its greatest peril.

Stability can become routine and mundane, causing you to be taken for granted by your superiors. If you're in an "up or out" company, you may not be able to hold the job for long without coming under close scrutiny from your superiors.

Breakpoint Signals

The internal breakpoint signals: your own feelings about your job and who the "enemy" is. If it's "us versus top management (or upper management)," you're at a clear breakpoint in your attitude, whether your internal adversary relationship is justified or not.

Other *internal* breakpoint signals:

—"If they'd only let me alone I could do the job";

—the perceived need for more time to spend working with employees and less time on "wasted" paperwork and reports "nobody ever reads."

External breakpoint signals are also easy to ignore:

—missed meetings with your counterparts in other departments;

—changed group assignments where you're no longer included;

—reports and memos that once were routed to you as a matter of routine but you don't see anymore.

If you're looking for your freedom and independence and have resented these "interruptions" in your job, you're not likely to notice when they're gone.

Or if you do notice, you may be tempted to welcome them back.

Breakpoint Forces

Isolating yourself from other departments tends to make you "the forgotten man." It's one of the quickest ways to termination short of being caught misappropriating funds. Most organizations function best as a team, and though we'd all like to be the lone-operative James Bond type from time to time, there's little practical way this attitude can be sustained when working for the average profit-making organization.

If you isolate yourself from the herd, you forfeit the herd's protection.

There are no shortcuts to group involvement; unless you're prepared to play the organizational game, you may soon find yourself on the sidelines.

Breakpoint Strategy

The key is to *want* to be involved with other departments, even though you're not trying to rise above your own level.

Keep your goals focused on company objectives and think of yourself as a professional. Don't indulge in "us versus upper management" thinking.

You have professionalism, your home and family, and personal work satisfaction as motivational forces. Take advantage of them; everyone else does. After all, you're competing with everyone else, whether or not you want to move up.

Those below aspire to your job. To keep them motivated you must stay motivated by the rewards that doing good work at your chosen level can bring you.

Strive to be indispensable to your superiors and your fellow department heads by taking advantage of your position. Management needs to know what its people are thinking and you're the closest level most of your superiors are likely to get to "grass roots."

Be certain to provide consistent information about changing attitudes in your department toward various areas of company policy and other motivational "triggers" that upper-level management wants to "pull."

Make it a point to keep your own records from regular reports you get from subordinates on all aspects of your department's thinking. Jot down how subordinates view company products, how they want to spend their leisure time, what they think of the company's advertising, the company's policy toward maternity or paternity leaves, absenteeism, and so on. Keep tabs on their ambition by learning where they want to go on vacation, what kinds of cars and fashions they admire, and what kinds of neighborhoods they aspire to.

Each time your company wants to set a new policy or change an existing one, this kind of information will be invaluable—and so will you.

To avoid being "included out" of interdepartmental activity, keep a running list of each interdepartmental activity your predecessor and you have been involved with. When there's a change, point out the change to whoever is responsible. "I missed your usual memo on personnel recruiting last Monday," you might mention. "What's going on?" By mentioning it, you'll have shown your interest, and even if you've been excluded from this category for one reason or another, the odds are that some other activity will arise for you. Keep track of the game schedule and the rosters, so you don't find yourself permanently benched.

POLITICAL BREAKPOINTS

An executive we'll call Bill Dunham headed up three accounting departments in a southern district for a major canned-goods company and was well respected. His work and that of his departments was consistently good. He stayed on top of his deadlines and met all of his firm's objectives. At age forty-two, he was offered the post of division accounting manager with a 20 percent jump in salary and a move to the regional office in Atlanta from his home in Charleston. Bill had two children in high school at the time, and his wife didn't want to move. After long and serious thought, he turned down the offer.

Within the next several months, Bill noticed a gradual change in his work patterns. Departments that had previously been prompt in providing his department with their results now became less so. Some of the reports he received were not in final form and others were incomplete. His staff members complained of the relatively sudden lack of cooperation and began using the shortcomings of others as an excuse for lassitude. Within six months, Bill realized that his department was no longer operating at the same standard of efficiency. The following quarterly review with Bill's newly appointed superior brought a mandate to turn things around in three months or face "further action."

Breakpoint Signals

Promptness is perhaps the first signal for spotting political cooperation or lack thereof. No manager has enough hours in the day, and it's inevitable that some of those we work with will be shortchanged. If you're among those who come up on the short end of your colleagues' time priority, you've got some political fence mending ahead of you.

Breakpoint Forces

Everyone, perhaps, likes a rising star. Everyone wants to believe in the coattail effect, and to think that they've picked a winner who will one day lift them up to bigger and better things—or who will at least protect them from hostile forces. When Bill turned down his promotion, his "rising star" charisma instantly faded. His colleagues no longer thought of him as evaluating the numbers passed up the line; they now viewed him as a number cruncher and a pencil pusher. His own staff caught the disease of disrespect and began seeing other department heads as more powerful than theirs, not to mention that they may have felt blocked from promotion by a boss who would not move.

Breakpoint Strategy

We all work for something. Recognize what your function does to assist other departments and be clear in communicating exactly why each department needs to cooperate.

Think of ways to develop good political relations with peer managers. Each time you have an opportunity to mention their work to a superior, let them know about it, and they'll soon realize that your opinions have effect beyond your level.

Outside the workplace, you may also have some ways to help your colleagues, who in turn will be likely to show their appreciation. One department head at a major consumer products company in New York has held the same spot for twenty years. He's seen many a rising star come and go and has maintained the best possible relations with all. His secret? He knows the maître d's at five of the city's top restaurants—knowledge he updates from time to time with renewed visits and fifty-dollar bills passed to keep relations current. His name can guarantee a seat. "Each of the other managers could probably do the same if they put their minds to it," he recounted once with a chuckle, "but they aren't around long enough to think about these things."

If you put your mind to it, you can probably think of ways you can provide "fringe benefits" to others at your level. You needn't offer services directly; it's more effective if you just mention from time to time what you've done for someone else and allow the implication to stand that you can provide valuable tips for those who cooperate with you.

Occasionally you'll meet an adversary who couldn't care less about whether your department and his see eye to eye. There may even be an attempt to become established in the pecking order by putting your department down. Although such tactics will not be likely to further individual goals, they can't be left unchallenged or your own department image will suffer.

A public challenge must usually be responded to publicly. Expect the worst from signals you get indirectly—indirect warnings of this kind of "hot dog" behavior. Attempt to establish agreement privately about the various forms of sniping, but the next time you're in a meeting with the "hot dog," be ready with an even-tempered but crisp rebuttal. Don't think that you can "sort things out in private" the way you can with a subordinate. With this type of opponent, very little that's said between you in private will matter because this is a judgment issue. The odds are he/she won't want to bother meeting privately with you in the first place. Accordingly, you've got to go public.

The first step is a quiet one-on-one with each of your other department heads. "Are you having trouble with X? I don't know why he's got the attitude he can do everything by himself." This kind of remark may elicit support and uncover other instances of non-cooperation.

You then can take the more effective route of bringing up the lack of cooperation on a general or at least more than one departmental level at your next group meeting. Or, if that fails, you can make a "paper trail" of memoranda from various department heads to the one miscreant with copies to the division head. There can be no "live and let live" when you're confronted with this kind of individual.

You've got to take the time and energy to fight back. To take a passive role is to risk the misinterpretation of everything you do. The miscreant will spread a tale of "trying to get something accomplished without a lot of interference from those do-nothings in department X," and eventually people will believe what's being said. If your company offers conflict resolution as a service, where an outside impartial consultant is brought in, perhaps you may want to go this route.

SPECIAL POINTERS

Non-verbal Signals

In trying to move up the managerial ladder, many people are hampered by mannerisms that indicate they're susceptible to being "pushed around." Here are some body-language traits you need to develop in order to convey an impression that you're ready for a leadership position.

1. The military calls it "command posture." Sit with your head and shoulders at attention. Tilting your head, for instance, can be viewed as a submissive gesture where you may come across as someone easily swayed, even though you may simply be trying to show empathy.
2. The military calls it "command presence." Don't smile unless you find something genuinely humorous to smile about. A strictly-business attitude will allow you to be respected rather than admired for your looks or personality. The latter may not get you promoted.
3. "Looking in the eye." The straightforward direct eye contact is de rigueur for authority. If you give your commands while looking at the floor or at the walls, you won't find many responding with obedience or interest.
4. Don't reinforce your counterpart's conversation by nodding. Emulate the Buddha. To nod overfrequently is to give the impression that you're agreeable, perhaps sending a mixed message if in fact you don't agree. In managerial circles, it's difficult to say "yes" much of the time.
5. Develop the "command voice." You don't get paid to be a soft-spoken, shy wallflower in business. Nor will you last long if you sound shrill. Practice speaking aloud about the most painfully sensitive work-oriented subjects you can think of until you can control your voice to project a feeling of quiet acceptance and confidence. Take time in privacy to work with a tape recorder. Though you may find it embarrassing at first, you won't regret the hours spent developing this key trait. When you can step into a situation without a tremor,

you'll be taken seriously. Until that time, no matter what you say, you'll have difficulty making a strong impression.

Point to Remember: Various psychological studies have indicated that people rarely remember exact words. The impact from a speaker comes predominantly from how he or she looks, with dress and body-language traits most important. The sound of the person's voice, the tone of assurance or other appropriate emotion, makes up about 40 percent of the impact. Less than 10 percent of the overall impression comes from the words themselves.

It's up to you to make certain that the key 90 percent works in your favor. Practice, practice, practice.

CHANCE TO MOVE

As a mid-level manager on the steady path, you should be aware that the choice offered you may be a "stepping-stone" kind of position, and that once you take it you'll have committed yourself to an "up or out" career path. To recognize this kind of position, determine:

1. Who held it before, for how long, and whether they've moved up or out. If the new job fills a retiree's shoes, the move may work out, unless changing conditions have forced the man's retirement or have changed the character of the job to one of less critical importance.
2. What kind of visibility will you have? If you're going abroad at this level, you can almost guarantee that few in the home office will remember you when you return. They'll remember the head of your foreign office, though, since that's who sends home the reports. You thus become more vulnerable to the personal preferences of the head of your foreign office and can quickly find yourself without job security. A good general rule at this career stage is that unless the foreign chief has asked for you personally and has reason to know of your work, don't go.

Chapter 10

Middle Management
Fast Track

Capsule Summary

Though you're 100 percent dedicated to the corner-office goal, pay attention to the advice in the previous chapter. The productivity problems your steady-path counterpart has are yours as well. So, too, are the political needs to protect your department's integrity.

But on the fast track, it's not enough to perform acceptably in meeting your production objectives. You've got to show you have what it takes for the corner office well in advance of the time you're ready—and well in advance of the time when management will *listen* to you on key subjects such as company policy and corporate personnel development.

To distinguish yourself as one in the corner-office mold, look beyond day-to-day requirements of your job and demonstrate excellence in your own backyard and fresh ideas about everyone else's business. This may be the ideal time to consider the outside PR help we discussed earlier. The strain, particularly when you haven't been around long enough to know all the answers, can burn you out quickly. Or jealous colleagues can torpedo your career ship.

PERFORMANCE BREAKPOINTS

An executive we'll call Fran had her rising star tarnished in a way she hadn't anticipated. Manager of an old, well-established hotel that had been newly bought out and made part of a chain, she improved the occupancy level and profitability by nearly 25 percent during her first three years on the job. Then trouble arose when two of her department heads announced they were getting married and leaving the company. She was caught without a replacement, and had to ask for time to recruit and interview from other locations.

The hotel's policy was to promote from within, and inside the chain a candidate was soon found. During this process Fran's image as a "people developer" suffered with her superiors, and she lost a great deal of empathy from the employees in her hotel who had been passed over.

While management intellectually understood, it didn't matter that twin resignations were unexpected. Fran hadn't been prepared, and the message seemed clear to subordinates that she wasn't considering them for promotion.

Worse, her superiors thought less of her as a leader and soon asserted that the 25 percent improvement in the bottom line had been due to company policies rather than her implementation and effective management.

Breakpoint Signals

An often overlooked maxim on the fast track is that you rise on the shoulders of others. Your subordinates, in turn, send signals to you about their needs and what you can do to fill them.

Fran later remembered that several times during the past two years her two key subordinates had each asked for a meeting with her specifically to discuss the company career plans for employees throughout the national chain. Since the company had no plans for cross-transfer between hotel units, Fran didn't want to seem empty-handed during such a meeting, so she regularly put it off.

Now she recognizes that the top employees' concern for "their subordinates" was probably a first step toward expressing concern for their own future career development.

Breakpoint Forces

If you're on the fast track, you may be younger than many of your subordinates. You'll certainly have more demands on your time than they, because in addition to mastering your job you'll be looking ahead to other departments and absorbing a wider range of information.

Those under you will recognize these demands even if it's only to think that you're "too busy" to give them much of your time. If you don't hear "cries in the night" from your subordinates, you may make the mistake of thinking they're happy in their work and can be taken for granted.

Remember, people at all levels need goals and a sense of belonging. In addition to the need for salary, status, professionalism, and other personal satisfaction, people need the security of knowing that their boss cares about *them* and their careers. Even those who have little direct contact with you will treasure the belief that if the chips are down you'll take an interest in their problems.

Don't disappoint your people in this basic human expectation.

Breakpoint Strategy

Make time to socialize. Ask about family, friends, community activities, sports events, and other general-interest matters. By establishing your own interest in non-work matters, you convey the message that your subordinates can get to you and let you know of their personal plans and needs.

Knowing that you have an interest in them, they'll be less likely to "include you out" of their future planning.

If possible, try to maintain the initiative for these talks and maintain proper perspective.

One caution: Once you have established good dialogue with your subordinates and peers you'll probably find that you could be spending an inordinate amount of time on "their" problems.

People have a way of gravitating to problem solvers, particularly if they think the problem solver enjoys being asked for advice. At the point you feel you're being taken advantage of, however, you may find it difficult to pull back. If those coming to you with problems feel put off, you run the risk of offending them.

Several years ago we had a consultant in our organization who was clearly one of the most popular people in the company. If anyone had a problem of any kind, he was there to help. So much was this the case that his performance declined and he suffered from loss of respect. Anyone whose time is others' time, subjects himself to others' managing that time.

Keep things on track and offer to help people work through problems rather than solving them for people outright. The associate in our firm finally described himself as being nibbled to death by ducks.

OTHER PERFORMANCE BREAKPOINT SIGNALS: THE PRESIDENT'S ROLODEX

A client we'll call Jim Connors was a well-respected department head in a major food-production corporation. His boss, the general manager, had been burned early in his career by a regulatory agency and was perhaps paranoid whenever the subject arose. When Jim approached the "normal" time for promotion, he knew that he was solid in every area of his own department and had enjoyed strong success during his tenure as manager.

Then one day in a conversation with his boss, he proposed a new idea and his boss responded with "Sounds interesting, but what do you suppose Fred Cavanaugh would think of it?"

Jim drew a complete blank—he'd never heard of Fred Cavanaugh—but his instincts told him he was on important ground. Instead of asking, "Who's he?" as he might normally have done, Jim said, "I haven't checked him out, but I can have a pretty good educated guess in the next two weeks if you're interested." He got a nod from the general manager.

After hours, Jim checked the telephone index on the desk of his boss's secretary. He discovered that Fred Cavanaugh was the FDA official assigned to monitor the company's advertising and marketing claims—an area with which Jim had had no concern in his production capacity up till now. A quick request to the company's legal department from Jim provided the FDA's precedents on the marketing of low-cholesterol products like the one Jim was proposing for production.

Jim didn't stop with the FDA. Using sources he had in other departments to get the appropriate names and phone numbers, he took some time to draw up a "cast of characters" who would be involved in a decision to produce and market the new product.

He presented the "cast of characters" to his boss with his report, at one stroke demonstrating an awareness of wider perspective required for the general manager's position and willingness to do the legwork.

Within six months he had his promotion.

Breakpoint Forces

Remember that passion for the "big picture" resolves itself into thousands of variegated details. It's not enough simply to discuss foreign policy or world economic affairs to show that you're looking upward and outward. Take the time to learn who and what outside factors are important to your superiors and you'll have the pattern of your future activities laid out for you.

Breakpoint Strategy

The president's Rolodex is an obvious example of a company's "cast of characters." Of course we don't recommend that you try to get unauthorized access to this information. Not only could you raise problems with security and invasion of privacy, but the odds are strong that you'd have no use for most of the president's contacts at this stage in your career. A better alternative would be to ask the boss's secretary for a list of the names and numbers that fit valuable business categories where you should make contacts and know who is important.

Your boss's Rolodex and phone logs are a valuable source of contacts. Other good sources: vendors and suppliers who are paid to deal with your company's problems and questions as well as problems and questions of competitors.

You can learn much from these "free consultants," but don't make heavy-handed shows of pitting one against the other, or hint at business you don't have the authority to generate. This last tactic can prove disastrous if word gets back to your boss that you're exceeding your authority and committing company reputation and goodwill without approval.

A recommended tactic: Tell vendors you're surveying the market for whatever item you seek to acquire and you want to know whether they have systems in place with any of your competitors. Your discussion with those who have made sales to your competitors will often turn up information about their satisfaction with the new equipment and about their plans and problems.

Knowing the "inside" of the competition may give you a leg up on your competitors within your company.

PERSONAL BREAKPOINTS

Breakpoint Signals

Much has been written about the "burnout-dropout" phenomenon among fast-track managers. You're probably aware of all kinds of symptoms and of remedies ranging from high-tech exercise equipment to tropical vacations complete with low-calorie yogurt diets.

One factor we've noticed among "burnout" clients who come to us at G&S is what we call the "too much too soon" phenomenon.

At the risk of appearing to contradict ourselves, this cause of burnout is often directly attributable to advice we just gave in the preceding section: that to stay on the fast track, you've got to look outward as well as upward. Many fast-track mid-level managers try to give 100 percent of their effort in all directions.

The 100 percent is what's wrong with this strategy.

In other words, burnout often results from trying to do and learn too much too soon. Pace yourself.

Breakpoint Forces

No one can be all things to all people. This applies to company presidents as well as to fast-track mid-level managers who aspire to become company presidents.

Remember that the company president has a support network at work where the mid-level manager works largely as an independent. All too frequently, the mid-level manager doesn't have either the experience or the power base to cope with demands made from those beneath and above.

What happens?

Usually, they fake it. Not wanting to appear less than presidential, the manager often makes promises that are difficult to keep, thus is forced to operate in doubt in areas that should have been investigated before leaping in.

The strain of maintaining an illusion of omnipotence sooner or later will catch up, resulting in "projection" of fatigue and unhappiness into the work environment.

Goals often become "worthless" in an emotional sense, and resulting cynicism can become a trait too readily seen in others.

The result: Work then becomes a chore and the balance of the burnout symptoms—loss of appetite, depression, and family tensions—can quickly follow.

Breakpoint Strategy

Don't think that to avoid illusions of omnipotence and the consequent dangers you've got to act subservient.

Use the prerogatives and perquisites at your level to ask questions rather than pretend to have answers.

Just asking, "What do you suggest?" or "What would you rather do?" can take the burden off your shoulders and improve relations with the person you're asking—provided you don't overdo it.

When using this technique, however, be sure to accompany your request for recommendation with a request for backup data. Don't just ask, "Why do you think we should take this approach?" Ask instead, "Are there other ways to skin this cat that other people are going to question?" And then, "What kind of supporting data should we have on hand to convince people of our choice?" By using these three questions judiciously, you'll have learned what you need to know with a minimum of strain.

You then can ask the fourth question, "Who's going to put the data together?" to complete the process.

The key to employing this questioning technique, however, is your *attitude*. The way you ask the questions must imply: "I don't have all the answers and I need your help to formulate a decision."

If you ask these questions in an authoritarian manner that implies you've got your mind made up and are just testing the other party, you'll be back in the same mode of omnipotence and stress pattern. You won't get the same quality of answers using intimidating tactics, and you may generate ill will and resentment.

POLITICAL BREAKPOINTS

The mid-level fast-track area is the most widely publicized "dog eat dog" political environment.

For good reason.

The numbers alone make it apparent that of every twenty-five mid-level managers, only one will move up to the general manager level. When you consider that performance skills have brought each person up to the mid-level range and that the general manager performance skills aren't overwhelmingly difficult to learn, you can see that performance alone is not going to ensure your promotion.

The result, regrettably, is that many managers become excessively possessive and develop a "cutthroat" attitude. Competitive fears feed on themselves when concentrated internally and eventually affect performance.

Oddly enough, a cutthroat atmosphere can provide you with an excellent political opportunity.

Breakpoint Signal 1

All the political messages you've read about for your steady-path mid-level counterpart apply to you as a fast-track candidate.

Adversarial interdepartmental meetings can be symptomatic of more than everyday conflicts between departments. If your department is having difficulty with others, it may be that you've acquired a political adversary without knowing it.

Breakpoint Strategy

Take time to uncover the source of your political difficulty if at all possible and use some symbolic opportunity to demonstrate that you bear no ill will toward any individual. You might, for instance, have your department "go the extra mile" to provide assistance to the adversarial department. *But* "go the extra mile" for the adversary only after you've "gone the extra mile" for other departments whose political allegiance you already have.

By so doing, you send a clear message that your goals are to improve company-wide practices and environment and that you have not been coerced into showing favoritism to the offending party.

Perhaps just as important, you've reduced the negative effect of your detractor by the value you've added to those who support you. "After all, he can't be as bad as X makes him out to be," they'll think. "He certainly is taking care of my end of things well enough."

Breakpoint Signal 2: "Johnny-come-lately"

One of the most frequent fast-track political pitfalls comes from disrespect shown to younger rising stars by more experienced and jealous colleagues.

Breakpoint Forces

Part of this hostility is natural, of course, since it comes from a competitive drive from within.

Another part is personal antagonism that comes from being regarded as too wrapped up in your own concerns to notice employee needs. This can be dealt with using the strategy we've just described: producing for them.

Breakpoint Strategy

By demonstrating your capacity to fill their requirements and help meet their needs, you will show that your abilities deserve respect.

To legitimize your "rising star" image, nothing succeeds like positive publicity. We're not talking about "house organ" notices of your on-the-job activities, because the mid-level stage is the point where professional performance at industry conventions and regional associations becomes a necessity, rather than a device to separate yourself from others at the level you've just left.

Take time to cultivate media outside your professional area. Local radio stations and local cable TV stations are constantly searching for talent to fill air time. Try to pick media that will reach a target audience that's likely to be respected by your superiors. Supply programming suggestions and a brief vita that demonstrates your capability to provide interesting information in an area *indirectly* related to your work activity.

Why indirectly? You don't want to expose yourself to confidential questions about your company's future plans; rather, position yourself to make constructive commentary about areas in which you've got a legitimate right to be treated as an authority.

If areas indirectly related to your business activity aren't "salable" or are too sensitive for you to risk going public, stick to those topics you can comment on safely: family, friendships, personal values, work ethics, tax programs, regional "boosterism," and the like.

When you're on the air, remember that 90 percent of your impact comes from non-verbal presentation. If it's television, videotape yourself prior to your appearance to get a good look at your body language as well as the effect of your clothing on the program's context. If it's radio, tape-record questions and answers constantly to capture the tone and style of response, the two factors your audience is most likely to remember.

A last step to take prior to going on the air: Mention to your immediate superior that you've been asked to appear on the XYZ panel show; ask whether there are any problem areas you ought to avoid. Have in mind, when you ask, what problem areas are likely to arise, then add, "It strikes me that I'd better avoid any reference to [whatever work areas you think are sensitive], but I've been assured that these topics aren't likely to come up."

Don't overlook this last step. If nothing else, it makes your boss aware that you're considered worth public attention. Otherwise, you have no assurance that anyone in your company will actually see or hear your performance.

Breakpoint Signal 3: "The Poisoned Plum"

An executive we'll call Matt Brandon was pleased when his boss offered a new "extracurricular assignment" heading a committee on shareowner relations. The boss explained that Matt's predecessor had become too wrapped up in a special project to continue, and that Matt's acceptance of the post would give upper management the chance to see how he performed in a critical public relations function.

Matt accepted with enthusiasm. He picked up the prior committee's minutes and shareowner-contact materials, and set up an initial conference with his fellow committee members. His agenda was well thought out and in accord with the previous month's efforts. At this first meeting, the shareowner-contact program previously under study was fully ratified by the group and Matt took action to set the program in motion at full speed.

Within the next two months, however, the company's third-quarter report came out, showing that profits had taken a nosedive. The company's major competitor brought out a lower-priced, higher-quality version of his company's product. Stock prices tumbled. Matt later recounted, "I was set up from the start. My predecessor knew what was coming and wanted someone else to take the heat when the bottom fell out. I wish I'd looked around before leaping into that committee chair."

Of course, there was nothing Matt or his committee could have done to prevent the stock decline and the accompanying high index of dissatisfaction that his shareowner-contact program uncovered. However, by looking ahead to see what might go wrong, Matt might have paved the way for a better defensive strategy in dealing with shareholders, or at least positioned his committee operations as defensive efforts in the eyes of his superiors.

Breakpoint Forces

No company expects a 100 percent success rate with each of its projects, and some weak spots are more readily detected than others.

Breakpoint Strategy

Be wary of new assignments and be quick to analyze the worst that can happen—a failure projection even while making plans to achieve the best.

Another wise strategy is to have ready a series of pet projects you'd like to undertake. That way, if you're offered a "poisoned plum," you can try to gracefully sidestep with an alternative that you can justifiably recommend as being more to your interest.

Remember, rejecting any assignment puts you on sensitive ground, particularly when the assignment comes from your boss. Be extra careful not to give any impression of challenging authority.

A CHANCE TO MOVE

Outside Your Company

At G&S the maxim we recommend for evaluating fast-track mid-level opportunities is: "Look out for number one."

By "number one," we don't mean just you, however. Be sure either that the company you're going with is number one in your area of expertise or that your area of expertise is a top concern for that company's success.

With either or both of these criteria fulfilled, you can be assured that your new assignment will keep you on the fast track. Either you'll be exposed to greater levels of responsibility at a company where your area is of critical importance, or you'll be able to use the new company's top reputation for training purposes and as valuable data for your résumé if and when you eventually move again.

In a recent survey of managers, we found that the average manager will change jobs three to four times in a thirty-year career.

Within Your Company

For intra-company moves, first evaluate what you're being offered with a "poisoned plum" attitude. How could this job cause me to fail? Since the move will affect the family, ask for time to talk it over with your family, then during that brief interval go hammer and tong at investigating the chance for success.

Consider not only the track record of your predecessor but also regional differences that may become critical to your personal performance. Can you live with the values and tastes of the new region? Can you use your techniques to motivate the on-site work force? Are your own personal tastes and mannerisms likely to brand you as a "tenderfoot"? Will you be able to overcome this initial response? Remember that your ability to broaden your appeal and diversify your strengths is a key to fast-track advancement—you'll see that the problem areas relating to geographic differences are really opportunities in disguise.

If you're dead certain you can't overcome these problems, however, turn down the assignment for "family reasons," and investigate other opportunities within or outside your company. Don't forget that refusing a move is a quick ticket off the fast track in many organizations.

The Move Abroad

From the mid-level fast-track position, you may get an opportunity to head up a foreign satellite or subsidiary division at the general manager level. This opportunity should be evaluated in the usual manner you apply to foreign moves (see the "A Chance to Move" material in Chapter 6). More important, however, evaluate the move in terms of the recognition you'll be able to attain.

If your *only* objection is that you may not be noticed by top management for the next two or three years, think twice before refusing. As a mid-level executive committed to the fast track, you have already dramatically limited your options to turn down offers of transfer, for all the "broadening" and "company loyalty" reasons we've mentioned in this and preceding chapters. Your efforts here should be like Matt's in making advance preparations for foreseeable and foreseen problems.

If isolation and exposure are the main drawbacks, act before you leave. Set up reporting procedures that ensure you'll be noticed at regular intervals.

Or negotiate internally for increased authority to evaluate and if necessary terminate local personnel, if it appears that the foreign office is not up to standard. Remember, you're much more likely to be granted increased authority before you take the job than once you've arrived. If increased authority isn't granted in advance, you've laid the groundwork to repeat requests for that authority in the future, and to explain what may go wrong without the attendant power base.

SPECIAL POINTERS

Breakpoint Forces

In today's job market, more people of varying backgrounds are moving up—and the competition is tougher. During the initial flurry to act affirmatively, the more assertive individuals often moved up first, among them the fast talkers who promised the moon. Your company may have suffered when the early promotions of big talkers turned sour. Accordingly, your company may be wary of those who promise more than they deliver.

Breakpoint Strategy

Create a commitments calendar. Many computer programs will automatically remind you of project due dates, but you needn't have a PC on your desk to develop an efficient reminder system. The calendar on your desk will work just fine, as will your personal desk-side file bin with folders for each day of the week or each day of the month, where you can put correspondence or memos that must be dealt with on each day. Don't try to delegate this kind of filing to your secretary, who may have difficulty setting priorities for these tasks.

Whatever system you use, the key to success is to build in stages of pre-deadline deadlines. Remind yourself not only of the deadlines you need to meet but also of checkpoint dates in advance of each deadline. Remind yourself of obstacles you'll encounter to reach your project goal on time.

Also build in an "early-warning system" for your superiors, to post them on how you're progressing. If you're going to be on schedule, say so before they ask. If you're not going to be on schedule, also say so before they ask. The second trait will win you more points than the first—though you'll need a clear explanation of what caused the delay and what you're doing to counter it.

The net result will be a sense among your superiors that you can be depended on, always a key ingredient to an upward move.

Chapter 11

General Manager
Steady Path

Capsule Summary

The general manager post puts you at the top of day-to-day operations in your management area or geographic region. Traditionally, you report directly to an officer of the company. In a large corporation, there are generally four or more layers of management between you and union-level, non-exempt-level workers on the production line. Some companies would call you a "senior-level" manager, but age is a lesser criterion than experience and performance today, particularly in high-tech areas or youth-oriented markets such as fast foods, franchise chains, or entertainment.

Your performance at this level is measured primarily by objective results produced largely by your subordinates. Your superior, the company officer, usually doesn't care how you get the job done; the numbers that go to the board of directors and ultimately the stockholders are most important.

Accordingly, your bonuses and raises may depend more on objective numbers and less on whether you've got the right "chemistry" or you're in the right country club or sending your kids to the right private school. At least, this will be the strong base of your employment contract, which you're likely to have at this level.

Within your operational domain, you are generally the last point of appeal for lower management, or if there is an appeal beyond you it is generally to a specialized personnel department in the home office. You have wide latitude determining who is hired and who is fired among your management subordinates.

In short, at this level you function as a regional company president in all areas except setting policy and raising capital. Paradoxically, it's this position of semi-omnipotence that's likely to present you with your greatest problems as a general manager if you've selected the steady path. You've got to avoid a defensive posture, even though you're dependent on those beneath you to maintain progress. You've got to maintain an objective attitude, even though you'll have more than your share of "family" ties between you and your subordinates.

Finally, to stay on the steady path, you've got to protect yourself against the ever-present "up or out" philosophy that's likely to be imposed when a new rising star appears at the company officer level. To be certain that your company doesn't go looking for "someone who can do more than just run the division," you can develop your natural advantages as a regional head by making yourself indispensable in the corporate relations with the other power centers in your area.

PERFORMANCE BREAKPOINTS

A former marketing manager we'll call Larry Swanson accepted the general manager job for the northwest region of his company, a shipbuilding-parts manufacturer, mainly because the move enabled him to return to Portland, Oregon, his hometown. He and his wife had always dreamed of settling there one day, and the promotion gave them everything they wanted—or so it seemed at first.

Within a year, though, Larry's dream job had turned to desperation. The recent economic slowdown had cut sales and production sharply, and the hometown friends and workers who had idolized Larry as a newly returned "hero" now were showing him all the fears of impending unemployment or salary cuts. After all, he was one of them; he was their natural advocate with the New York home office.

Adding to Larry's woes, a rebellion among several of his Young Turk and mid-level managers in the production area seemed to be brewing. The rebels were advocating a new high-tech production system as a cost-cutting and production benefit, and it was taking all Larry's efforts to hold them off.

"I didn't understand the technology, of course," Larry recalls, "but one thing I knew was that it was no time to be investing new capital while cutting jobs. I had all I could do to keep things afloat without rocking the boat making drastic moves."

What happened? The worst. Disaffected, the two Young Turks who'd dreamed up the new high-tech productivity system went with a competitor. The competitor was soon underpricing and outproducing Larry's company. The mid-level managers who had fought Larry for the change and lost were quick to say "I told you so," and let word spread back to the home office.

"Those guys didn't know what loyalty was," Larry moaned later. "They were outsiders and couldn't have cared less whether we kept people on the job or not."

Only after layoffs became necessary, due to the now reduced market share in good times, did Larry see that he was wrong. "I should have bitten the bullet when I had the chance," he says now. "I only postponed the pain and cost myself a job in the process."

Breakpoint Signals

As general manager, you'll be constantly bombarded with requests for change. As head of operations, you're the judge and jury for fledgling ideas —at least until your judgments are proven wrong. The breakpoint signal to learn to recognize, however, isn't the "we're behind the times" theme that always accompanies new ideas and recommendations for change.

What you need to recognize is your pattern of evaluation. Of the recommendations for change, how many are you turning down? How many are you seeking out? How many do you approve?

No matter what your business, if your initial response to suggestions for change is consistently negative, you are at a performance breakpoint.

If you haven't sought out on your own initiative new ideas for work-related change, you're also at a performance breakpoint.

Breakpoint Forces

As a general manager who's chosen the steady path, you have as your greatest adversary your own inertia and satisfaction with your present achievement. The status quo may be splendid, but it's your enemy if it has blinded you to the company's competitive position. If you don't strive to improve, your competitors will. In your position of authority you may have no direct supervisory force above you ensuring that you change with the times. Accordingly, you must be your own mentor for change.

Breakpoint Strategy

1. Keep a record of each change opportunity that crosses your desk and your response. In a separate monthly review, write out a one-page summary of the ideas and what you did with them.
2. Systematically cultivate outside contacts who can stimulate your creative thinking and report on new developments. A banker may be a particularly good source of data if his bank lends primarily to corporations similar to yours or has contacts in a field where similar innovations might apply.

Don't be shy about cultivating this relationship even if you are outside the capital formation or corporate borrowing decision-making process. As an area employer, you are an attractive target for any bank that can use savings of your employees, local checking purchasing account business, or refinancing company real estate in the area, even if it doesn't handle the corporate payroll.

A good bank is willing to invest and a commercial lender will see you as an "in" at the home office, where lending decisions for major production equipment or plant facilities will originate. Any banker will be happy to discuss advantages associated with these capital-intensive purchases.

Other sources to utilize systematically from outside are vendors and regulators, whom we've discussed in earlier chapters, particularly if your areas of opportunities for change involve purchase of new equipment. If your areas of change are people-intensive, involving organizational changes and personnel practices, you would do well to cultivate relationships with local politicians or attorneys who may be familiar with the positive and negative effects of such innovations, if any.

Other often overlooked sources of new ideas are public relations firms, who are paid to publicize what their clients have done to position themselves at the forefront of their industries. You may not get proprietary information or trade secrets this way, of course, but industrial espionage isn't what we're discussing here.

The important ingredient is your attitude on change and your ability to evaluate on an independent basis what flows upward from your subordinates to you. After all, you're paying your people to encourage ways to do the job better and cheaper; it's only right that they fulfill this responsibility and that you as manager of the interrelated innovations decide which priorities should be accepted and which should be saved for another time or discarded.

Henry Ford had the philosophy that no one had a corner on the new-ideas market. Though he had an extremely dominant personality, capable of withering the strongest opponent with his feisty retorts, he continually encouraged new ideas from workers.

In fact, at one point he set up a series of incentives for workers to come up with worthwhile ideas. The amount of money an idea saved or made for the company was used as the benchmark for the incentive. In some cases, workers took home a hefty check as a reward.

Needless to say, new ideas flowed freely through the system, and in the early days of production-line management, this resulted in the Ford production line being far more advanced than competition.

PERSONAL BREAKPOINTS: "IT MIGHT HAVE BEEN ME"

An executive we'll call Harry Hewitt reached his post as general manager in a large telecommunications company after twenty years with the organization. The regional office where he now assumed command was in Miami, where he and his second wife had spent many happy vacations. Another plus, or so it seemed at first, was that one of the district-level managers was John Hodges, an old college classmate and fraternity brother of Harry's. The two had kept in touch over the years on a Christmas-card basis, and their first meetings were all that Harry could have hoped for. John was quick to show that he understood that a level of management separated the two friends. "You don't have to worry about my trading on our friendship," John assured him. "I won't have anyone saying my promotions came from anything but my own merit."

Regrettably, it soon became apparent to Harry that John's personal life wasn't all it could have been. The couples exchanged dinner invitations, and the disarray in John's marriage was fairly clear. The obligatory social exchange didn't lead to further encounters between the couples, and Harry put the personal differences aside as he concentrated on work.

After a time he got wind of John's affair with one of the company secretaries, a former line operator who had risen to a position in the executive offices and still retained many friendships among the "girls on the line." At first Harry let the rumor lie, thinking it only gossip, until a union representative made a remark at a grievance-procedure meeting: "I guess Betty [the employee whose punishment the union was challenging] should have dyed her hair black."

Confronted with Harry's face-to-face demand for either a confirmation or a denial, John poured out a tale of woe. His wife was seeing a psychiatrist, he hadn't had a good physical relationship with her for nearly a decade, the brunette secretary he'd fallen in love with was the first person in years who'd made him feel "like a man." The news hit Harry hard, since he'd been through a similar experience with his own first marriage, although he hadn't looked to the women in his work-related world to provide the compassion lacking at home.

John pledged that he would end his affair, since he realized it was causing harm to the company, disrupting employee morale, and creating disrespect. He pleaded for time. Unwilling to seem callous, Harry nonetheless knew the only right decision was a quick, clean break, in spite of sympathy for his friend's situation. "You've got to make your choice here and now," he told John. "Either you stop seeing her or we meet to discuss your severance package." He and John agreed that the object of John's affections would be one of those secretaries transferred to another department within the next month as part of a division-wide rotational policy.

The following Friday, however, Harry dropped by the district office after lunch and discovered that John had taken the afternoon off and that the brunette secretary was also among the missing. A knowing smirk from others in the typing pool as Harry passed by the empty desk told him the worst. Embarrassed and angry and feeling as though he'd landed in the midst of a bad film, Harry nevertheless got the secretary's file from personnel, checked the address, and drove past on his way back to the division office. Sure enough, John's car was parked outside. Worse, he recognized two other line employees, both single women, as they emerged from the apartment house entrance and headed for the afternoon shift. No wonder John's affair had been so well known among the ladies, Harry thought to himself. Mentally, he forced himself to begin dictating John's termination notice and to go over the way he would present the matter to personnel. He began to formulate the recruiting plans for John's replacement.

Firing John subjected Harry to a barrage of emotions. John's wife tearfully pleaded: she could forgive him, why couldn't Harry and the company after all those long, hard years of service? The question haunted Harry during the weeks and months that followed, while John was unemployed. The cold realities of company policy seemed distant and meaningless compared to the heartbreak Harry knew John and his family were going through. If only he hadn't stopped by that one Friday. If only he'd given John another few days till the secretary's scheduled transfer. If only he'd let things slide or turned a blind eye. The "what if" questions haunted him.

In addition, he had to contend with underground resentment from many who felt that company policy had no business intruding into the personal lives of employees, and that the values Harry had displayed were not only outdated but intrusive. Harry had expected the second kind of criticism—he'd cleared the decision with company officers prior to terminating John—but his personal feelings made him less effective in defending his choice and the company's policy than he might have been. "That business with John set me back at least a year in terms of my getting a leadership handle on the division," he recounts. "It seems funny to say it now, but the sad part about it is that it *was* the right decision at the time, I *knew* it was the right decision, and I *still* didn't feel good about it. Worse, I let my feelings show and gave too many within the company the impression that I thought it was the wrong decision."

Breakpoint Signals

At the general manager level, "human values" will be all too readily apparent to ignore. Whether personal relations with your subordinates began before your work career or on the job, there will be strong tugs on your heartstrings whenever you contemplate any decision that you know will cause them pain.

Breakpoint Forces

You're now at a level where you've got to absorb opposing forces and maintain a consistent image—not to impress your superiors as a "comer," but to provide leadership to those who want and need the symbolic support of confidence "at the helm." If you allow yourself the luxury of showing personal feelings, you're headed for trouble.

Breakpoint Strategy

Accept in advance the inevitability of causing pain to those whose support and friendship you value. Organize your life, if possible, so that your emotional support from the workplace is strongly augmented by emotional support outside the job arena.

Like a professional actor, steep yourself in the role you know you must play and give the performance you know will be required of you as a leader. Take comfort in knowing that, according to study after study, firing a close associate is the single worst ordeal any executive has to go through. There isn't any painless way to make the break. You can make things a bit less painful by having the termination package and the severance paycheck ready at the time of the interview and by making certain that the terminated executive doesn't remain at the job site any longer than absolutely necessary.

If your company is in the position to use the services of an outplacement firm, you can lighten your day-to-day involvement with these matters and spare yourself the pain of reopening old wounds by having outplacement professionals handle the trauma and rebuilding process. You'll also most likely improve the odds of the terminated subordinate in getting rehired promptly. None of these measures, however, will insulate you completely from the pain of termination. Your best strategy is simply to exercise your willpower in resolving that the pain you feel won't interfere with your leadership performance. Key: Do what's right for the business.

POLITICAL BREAKPOINTS

In a sense, at the general manager level most of your breakpoints are "political," since so much of your job consists of motivating and managing people and the groups they make up. In the same sense, the kinds of breakpoints we've just described as "performance" or "personal" are also political, for these decisions have a direct effect on the general manager's political fortunes among subordinates.

The real "political" problem we've found faced by most executives who reached the general manager level on the steady path comes from above rather than below. We'll call it the "shake-up syndrome."

A typical "shake-up" has two players. First is the steady-path general manager who's running a well-managed division where there's been stability for the past three or four years. The other player is a newly arrived officer in the company, either from the ranks or from outside the company. Usually a fast-track candidate with an eye for the corner office, the new arrival knows he must make a mark as a decision maker if he's ever to be noticed. What easier opportunity than a well-run division? Much easier than tackling an area where things are not going well; there'd be some real problems to be handled in that instance.

So the heat goes to the well-run division.

Breakpoint Forces

The underlying motive of the new man, of course, is to replace or supersede the general manager with an "own team member," who can be counted on to provide support for continued upward move to the president's chair. Pure politics, of course. But knowing it's political doesn't stop this common process. As general manager, you aren't in a position to cry foul and base your trust on the president's sense of fair play. Remember, you don't have the president's ear the way the new man does, particularly if the president hired the new officer, unless he also hired you. You can be certain that the new officer's political clout is greater than yours if any "arguing the merits" is to be done.

Breakpoint Strategy

How do you protect yourself? Fight politics with politics, but choose the political arena that your adversary in the executive suite can't enter: the local level.

No company can afford to underestimate the importance of getting along in its local community at grass-roots levels, as countless labor strikes and regulatory horror stories have demonstrated. Take advantage of your natural constituency among local politicians, who will be more than appreciative of your implied endorsements for their candidacies by your employees, even though you can't do anything overt to express your support for them.

Schedule yourself with the other "outside" powers at the local level in direct proportion to their importance to the company. Some executives we know spend 20 percent of their time on "outside" contacts and feel that they've barely kept their fences mended. Only you can decide how much is required. Then, at every opportunity make the home office aware of how closely knit your regional political groups have become and, by implication, how difficult it would be for a new outsider to become established.

Political protection of the company's interests at the local level will protect your political interests at the home office. It's strong medicine to the threat of a "shake-up artist," who will be unable to match your powers on your political turf. Remember, many people within your organization are happy with you. They aren't interested in change any more than you are.

A CHANCE TO MOVE

At the general manager level, particularly if you become established and recognized, you're certain to become the target of executive recruiters. You'll receive telephone inquiries from legitimate companies who are under contract to fill a position and from operators who are trying to build a "stable" of candidates with the hope of finding one a vacancy to fill.

As a steady-path manager, you know your goals too well to leap at glittering promises of a future job paradise. Your first question could be on the tip of your tongue as you read this: How important is the position to be filled to the company that is looking?

Odds are, if the executive recruiter isn't a legitimate operator, he'll respond with the standard "Oh, it's a key position at your level; there's a good track from this spot to the home office." With this answer, we hope you know enough by now to hang up the phone. Similarly for such replies as "This is a young company that needs someone with your experience to set them straight in key areas." Or "The importance of your area to this company can't be overstated; that's why they're looking for someone of your caliber."

You know by now that these are exactly the job characteristics you want to avoid if you're committed to the steady path. This does not mean that you should never pursue such offers further, but initially, don't give them a second thought until you've reevaluated your career path using the "Test Yourself" materials we've provided for choosing between fast track and steady path. Also, don't make the traditional mid-forties mistake of equating fast-track job characteristics with macho power and lost youth. Visions of corporate jets and golden-parachute contracts shouldn't blind you to the realities of your own comfortable career goals.

Another rule when dealing with an executive recruiter: Volunteer nothing about your own career ambitions or qualifications in the first call. Find out more about your caller. Get the name and number of the recruiter's firm, find out how your name was selected, and ask for names of companies and contacts the recruiter has served in the past. If this information isn't forthcoming, terminate the call no matter how plausible the explanation. When you do get the names and phone number, check these names as you would check job candidate references before you return the recruiter's call. This way you'll be certain that you're dealing with a reputable firm and that you won't find your résumé being "floated" to other firms without your knowledge.

Four or five years ago, I met a senior-level manager from the Emery Company who felt that he had been set up, perhaps by someone in the company. After receiving a call from a headhunter, Ken decided to do up a résumé for what the headhunter had described as an ideal job, several levels higher and with more responsibility.

A short time after sending the résumé to the recruiter, Ken received a call from the head of personnel at the company. To make a long story short, somehow the company had gotten wind of the conversation and Ken's agreeing to compile a new résumé.

John Emery felt strongly that if someone was looking on the outside, he or she was disloyal, and he chose to fire the executive rather than discuss or question loyalty.

Was Ken set up? Perhaps, but we'll probably never know. Our point is: Know whom you're talking with and don't send your résumé to just anyone.

SPECIAL POINTERS

1. A positive management trait that takes many people to higher positions is an ability to develop talent. "Nurturing and developing strengths" may be your strong suit. If this is the case, firing a subordinate with whom you've come a long way will be particularly painful. There's no easy way to do it. To prepare yourself for such inevitable hard moments, you've got to steel yourself in advance, even when things are going beautifully. You must avoid the hesitancy, the urge to "let it ride" that may weaken your department and cost you the respect of both subordinates and superiors, as the executive we called Harry found to his regret.

2. A frequently publicized problem for people in upper management is the romantic subordinate. People are quick to gossip and are equally quick to presume the worst if they see what appears to be an especially close relationship between a superior and a subordinate of the

opposite sex. Notwithstanding this danger, a young subordinate may attempt to woo his or her way to a promotion. As a steady-path general manager, you may be more susceptible to "human relationships" on the job than your fast-track counterpart, who's more likely not to have time for that sort of thing—at least with subordinates. You may also be at a point in your career where your job has reached a plateau and you're subconciously looking for some excitement.

Don't fall for the romantic subordinate. Such affairs are not only dangerous but also extremely difficult to disentangle after an inevitable parting. Instead, concentrate on the positive achievements you want from life. Make your conquests job-related, not romantic.

3. We've noted in the main body of this chapter that your status as a steady-path general manager may leave you vulnerable to the "shake-up syndrome," and that an effective technique to combat unfair pressure from above is to show local political strength and indispensability at a manager's level. In today's politics, this may pose no greater problem for a woman executive than for her male counterpart, depending on the region of the country and the local politicians involved. However, in some areas, where the good ol' boys are in the seat of power, feminine status may prove to be a real political disadvantage.

If your position doesn't give you much hope of influencing city hall, you can still follow the same defensive strategy by taking a different tack. Instead of becoming the company's indispensable contact with the local governmental powers, identify other groups, both inside and outside the company, that are essential to the company's prosperity. Federal and state regulators are one group; local commercial leaders are another; a third might be church and civic leaders who influence your work force. Additionally, your company's top accounts and suppliers are another potential power base, though you're more likely to have already developed a strong business relationship with them by this point. Use all available resources at your disposal.

The basic technique is to identify a person or group that is indispensable to the company, and then show the company that you're indispensable to good relations and successful management of that person or group. You're in the driver's seat and have power.

CHECKLIST FOR SPOUSES

Reaching the general manager level means higher pay and other fringe benefits. It's a highly regarded, widely sought-after job. This is where salaries, bonuses, and options begin to escalate and where the payoff for long years of training and "working up" finally becomes more than a distant goal. There's a strong tendency to congratulate, celebrate, say "We've made it at last!" and get on with the business of living happily ever after. This may be the point where you want to enjoy your spouse's company, to relax, not to worry about money for the first time and just be comfortable.

Don't celebrate too soon. One of the prerequisites for staying at the general manager level is the ability not to be too comfortable on the job. Once your working spouse stops trying to improve things and no longer worries about what can be done to best competition, you're about to have career problems.

So don't become too comfortable. Control your leisure life so you're not interfering with the work that brought you to this level.

Above all, try not to make your spouse feel guilty about work. "I thought we were going to have such a good life when you got your promotion," or "I thought we'd have more time together," doesn't improve your relationship. If work has to be done, so be it. With the big job comes authority and responsibility. Responsibility takes time. You're much better off with a spouse who's not complacent at work, since complacent spouses won't be at work for long at the general manager level. Aggressiveness got them there; let their aggressiveness keep them there.

Also resist the urge to say "We're doing just fine, honey," with the implication that now there's no need for your spouse to take work seriously. Your spouse's satisfaction at work may extend beyond the monetary level you may have reached, for remember, your spouse has in all probability spent as much waking time or more on career development, as on your marriage. To trivialize your spouse's contribution, or to trivialize the efforts your spouse may be making to move ahead, can only harm your relationship or future.

Chapter 12

General Manager

Fast Track

Capsule Summary

As general manager on the fast track, you're exactly like your steady-path counterpart by being the on-site "president" of a small empire. Your performance has to be just as good as that of your steady-path counterpart, but additionally you've another audience to please: the executive-suite viewers who will be looking not only for performance and results from your division but also for visible indication that you've got the "leadership" necessary to rise further.

In addition, you've got to keep a weather eye on your company to see whether it's living up to *your* career needs. If your particular division isn't where the action is for the company, you're perhaps doing yourself a disservice every day you perform for them.

Also, though fatigue and jealousy may be taking their toll, you can't allow outside factors to overly affect your attitude toward competition and, especially, toward rising stars who are your subordinates.

You must take a cold look at social thresholds, especially those that stand between you and the executive suite. Regrettably, some first-rate general managers have been blocked from further advancement in eastern companies for simply not having attended a prep school. If there are cultural conflicts, recognize them and either correct, adapt, or depart without further ado.

Finally, as you're moving up, be alert to the trail you'll leave behind and be careful about the new territory you'll enter. In both instances, you can't depend on face value and good faith to avoid a career pitfall.

PERFORMANCE BREAKPOINTS

Breakpoint Signals

The opportunity seemed tailor-made for John. A whirlwind executive search had placed him at the head of the list of top candidates to replace an emerging company's hard-driving project manager, who had suffered a coronary and died. The company was eight months away from the scheduled introduction of a new food-processing product—one that would have excellent worldwide sales potential. John had full responsibility and credit for the introduction of a similar product—a sweetener production agent that had gained near-universal acceptance after a rather shaky beginning. John had "masterminded" the sales and marketing campaign and was acknowledged by his present company as the key man responsible for the "home run."

At the new company, the sales strategy was in shambles. John's unfortunate predecessor was a man with strong sales background, and had confidently postponed work on this part of the project while he concentrated on areas he considered to be weaker.

John took the reins in a climate of uncertainty but great hope. The sales manager who'd been selected by his predecessor looked to John with a mixture of awe and trepidation, having been on board only a month before the general manager's heart attack. "I'm certainly looking forward to working with a superstar," he said, grinning wryly. "Maybe I'll pick up some of your magic touch."

John knew not to take too much control away from his sales manager; after all, he credited much of his prior success to the general manager he'd worked under, who'd allowed him to go at his full potential and rewarded initiative rather than reactive programmed behavior.

The problem was that the sales manager hired for the job didn't have a background in planning or marketing. His strength lay in identifying good salesmen and motivating them. To his credit, John felt, the sales manager acknowledged this shortcoming, explaining that his predecessor had a marketing background and that he'd been chosen to complement his former boss's strength.

"No problem" was John's response. He dug out the prior campaign that had worked so well, and sat down to adapt it to the market they now faced. The two men worked extremely well together. By the time of introduction, they had lined up what John felt was a superb distribution team, and had a marketing strategy that John knew in his heart was better than the "home run" he'd hit for his previous employer.

But the new product bombed spectacularly. The first few shipments, having been stockpiled for several months, revealed a chemical engineering defect that no one had suspected. The "shelf life" in the eye-catching packaging John's group had designed was too short for some markets.

Most customers would have no problem, it turned out, but after a shipping delay combined with lag time in production longer than industry norms, a chemical breakdown occurred that rendered the product useless. Several major overseas customers lost large production runs before discovering this flaw. Of course, they didn't know the cause of the problem and didn't want to know. They simply voiced their displeasure and the word got around.

"By the time we identified the cause of the problem," John recounts, "the damage had been done. We put out a new campaign after we'd re-engineered and worked like crazy convincing people that what we were selling was 100 percent safe, and we doubled profits 200 percent, but nobody wanted to hear it." By then, a competitor had launched a similar product, capitalizing on the quality-control problem that John's product had acquired. "They used sales literature that would have done credit to a pharmaceutical house," John recalls without a smile. "And I would have done the same thing if I'd have been in their shoes. I'd have done it with a whoop of joy."

Breakpoint Forces

We all fall back on our strong points, a splendidly human characteristic, but in John's case it wasn't enough. As general manager responsible for all facets of a project, you must develop the quality of being everywhere at once, particularly where there is trouble.

In John's case, everyone on his team knew of his strength in sales, everyone on the team knew that sales was the key ingredient in the new product's success, and everyone relied on John's "home run" mystique.

The production manager who was responsible for "shelf life" matters didn't think to challenge the new packaging that John had recommended.

Of course, the production manager took some of the blame, but having a scapegoat gave John no comfort at all. Nor did it help repair John's tarnished reputation within his new company or the industry.

An opposite example of this came during the Tylenol poisoning crisis. Jim Burke, chairman of Johnson & Johnson, saw the need, the opportunity, and the problem. He immediately presented a strong leadership position by emphasizing quality and confidence in the brand in special advertising while he took immediate steps to develop a sealed container that is now prevalent in the industry. Before long he had turned a monumental problem for Johnson & Johnson into a personal victory.

The product rebounded strongly and Jim clearly emerged as a leader par excellence.

Breakpoint Strategy

Homilies about leaving no stones unturned and being systematic are a dime a dozen—but they're also true and in no case more so than for a general manager. As a fast-track candidate, you will be ruled in your upward drive by the pleasures of your past successes, and will be more likely to find yourself in unfamiliar situations, where the temptation to rely on your known strengths and skills is at its highest.

Steer clear of traps like the one that ensnared John. Sure, you want to power ahead with your own success fuel and you don't want to spread yourself too thin. But instead of being blinded by optimism, supplement your general manager's skills with what we at G&S call the failure projection.

The technique is simple. You draw up a list of everyone in your organization connected with the project or who might be connected with the project, and you note each person's function next to his or her name. Then, during one of your blackest moods, if possible, sit down and develop a list of each of the things each of the individuals could do to foul up the project. This list, of course, gives you a checklist of problems to safeguard against.

When you've completed your checklist on those within your organization, do the same exercise with those key to the project outside your organization. What would happen, for example, if two weeks before the closing of a major new acquisition your bank had a change of officers and refused to turn the solemn cocktail-party handshake you'd been given by your loan officer into a bona fide commitment? Sure, it's not likely and you've known the officer for ten years, but all the same, what if? Role-play, and with some practice you can put all your potential sleepless-night material on paper and institute safeguards to prevent each catastrophe.

Remember, if you're on the fast track, you're in a "diversity mode." You're also in a "crisis mode" whenever possible, since advancement depends upon your being a key player. Don't let natural optimism or the time pressures of a current crisis keep you from adapting multiple-perspective attention to detail required for diversification.

PERSONAL BREAKPOINTS: "KEEPING UP WITH THE OVAL OFFICE"

As a fast-track candidate, your instincts are to look upward and outward. What you'll see, of course, when you look up in your own company are the officers, who've probably been around the company longer than you and almost without question are making more money than you.

The temptation is to emulate their dress and whatever consumption they're most conspicuous at. After all, not only is it fun to own a Rolex and a Ferrari and watch the almost visceral impact these items have on their admirers; you're also trying to join an "in group." The first step to joining, as we all know from basic anthropology, is to symbolically appear in displays arrayed like "one of us."

Though at G&S we don't expect our advice to overwhelm a basic human need to display power totems, or to create much of a dent in the fine-watch and fast-car markets, we respectfully point out a few caveats that apply to any general manager tempted to buy his way into the executive suite.

One. If you're in a closely held company, the powers that be may be old money—with their own standards of what makes a person "one of us" and their own style of display that marks them apart from the rank and file or the "operations" people. In many cases, old money treasures old objects of value highly preserved, and your proud display of the latest Swiss chronometer would be a costly error, assuming that your audience in the executive suite was susceptible to such visual blandishments in the first place.

Two. We hasten to point out that any display at work is seen not only by those above you but also by those who report to you. If you've been trying to keep labor costs down, think of the effect your purchase of a $5,000 hand-tooled Parker shotgun for a hobby of pheasant hunting will have on subordinates who are trying to make the payments on their Datsun sedans. Think also of the hay your union rep can make with such symbolic purchases as he or she tries to isolate you from the rank and file.

Three. We respectfully suggest that what a company officer may find affordable on his salary and bonus—and on his wife's trust fund income—may put a strain on your budget. The result will soon make itself felt in the day-to-day attitude of your spouse and children, possibly as haunted disillusionment when bills are due or possibly as a raging desire to acquire more and more to be *really* in with the people they emulate. In neither case is the emotional carryover likely to benefit your own attitude or performance.

Four. If you're in a publicly held company odds are that conspicuous consumption by officers is frowned upon. Or if the officers indulge, they may jealousy guard this perquisite with an unwritten resistance to seeing it acquired by anyone beneath them. You may brand yourself as a "social climber" and be shunned; you may also brand yourself as an irresponsible profligate whose hands must be kept at all costs from the company's purse strings.

Five. In spite of this, you must maintain standards. In your company culture, of course, open collars and jeans may be de rigueur among the officers, particularly if you're in Silicon Valley. Throughout most of middle America, you'll be safe with the best level Brooks Brothers offers, and would do well to avoid "flash" items of jewelry that would be considered appropriate in New York. Other companies, particularly on the West Coast, will separate officer-level material from those more suited to remain in the "operational ranks" by whether or not the suits appear hand-tailored and the shirts custom-fitted. In this unfair world, officers are free to elevate a man or woman on the strength or weakness of barrel cuffs versus French, continental shoes versus wing-tips, Mont Blanc pens versus Dixon #2 soft leads.

Style preferences that are so emotional aren't likely to be stated. It's up to you to survey the field and make your best guess.

I recall a meeting I attended at General Foods a number of years ago in the old Kool-Aid division. The first person I met was the division manager. He was wearing a blue pin-striped suit, white shirt, blue rep tie, and black wing-tipped shoes. Not unusual dress by any standard, but what I did notice was that as we spoke he put his feet up on the desk and smoked a thin cigar.

I had four meetings subsequent to meeting the division manager, and you guessed it. All four men were dressed in blue suit, white shirt, etc., sat with their feet on the desk, and smoked thin cigars. Fortunately, role playing to this degree is not necessary or desirable at most companies.

Six. One final piece of advice: While balance is key, if the question is whether to put the money into your jewelry and wardrobe or into your "go to hell" fund, we recommend the latter. It's likely to give you just as much inner confidence, which you can depend upon as a hedge against the vagaries of boardroom taste.

POLITICAL BREAKPOINTS

You're about to move up the ladder and you know you don't have control over the choice of your replacement.

Breakpoint Forces

"The evil that men do lives after them, the good is oft interred with their bones." Shakespeare's gloomy truism isn't often quoted in the corporate world, but it's an apt description of the trail that's likely to follow you if your successor isn't competent and needs a scapegoat.

"Look at the mess I inherited," he or she will say, and go on to recount the "hidden defects" you left behind, hinting darkly that others still lie undiscovered and that he or she is the only one with the zeal and energy required to bring them to the surface.

This kind of finger-pointing is easiest and most prevalent when someone has left the company, but it can also occur with a geographical transfer, when the departed party isn't around to hear the scurrilous stories being spread.

Of course, the world would be a better place if the finger-pointing energies were directed into more constructive channels. But then again, human nature isn't likely to be radically altered between the time you read this and the time you make your next move up.

Breakpoint Strategy

Take inventory of the *continuing* projects you can renew or extend during your last months or weeks on the job. If there are good vendors whose contracts aren't up for renewal for another six months, for instance, renegotiate early. If there's legal action you've been deferring, begin action; if it's been ongoing and you think it's going nowhere, settle up. If there are promotions within your power to make, make them (it goes without saying, of course, that you sincerely believe the promotions are well founded).

In this fashion, you've made things easier for your replacement with fewer initial decisions to make. And you've also made failure somewhat less likely, which means that you've also protected yourself a little more from an attempt to blame such failure on you.

Don't, however, make the mistake of initiating a major new project within the final weeks or months of your time in office. Such efforts are usually doomed, even if they're as meritorious as tax reform.

Your replacement won't have much interest in parenting your brain-child. Why bother? After all, you'll be given the credit as a visionary if the project succeeds. If it flops there will be association with failure.

You *might*, however, leave plans for the idea on paper in a well-developed, easy-to-follow outline that hasn't been "shopped" around upper-level management for funding approval. If comfortable, your successor will be the originating sponsor of the idea, and will be motivated to see it through to completion. It's also less work for you.

Bigger Mistake: Putting friends or relatives on the payroll. You may think the world of them and know they'd do a super job. You may even be sure you can keep a required businesslike distance between them and you. *But as a fast-track executive, you must keep yourself free to move.*

Even if the people you recommended were right for the job, your personal relationship with them will be sure to cause resentment. Once you're gone, there'll be no one to protect them. They will be seen as a threat and their work lives will most likely become difficult if not impossible. Also, why run the risk of a hint of impropriety associated with nepotism which would be grist for your replacement's rumor mill?

A similar warning often applies to hiring people with whom your firm has had a prior business relationship, such as a current employee of a client or customer. Hiring a client employee can put the company relationship in jeopardy—in theory if not in reality.

Will the former employer be magnanimous about the loss of its employee? Perhaps. Could the "inside" experience the new employee gets with your firm be described in minute detail to the former employee's boardroom without a hint of embarrassment to your firm? Perhaps.

But there's no way to be certain that the reverse will not occur. However the relationship deteriorates, your hiring decision becomes an obvious scapegoat. You could be blamed if the customer company hardens its bargaining position on the next contract, holding out for a rate that's only marginally profitable for your firm. "How did they know our limits?" people may ask—and they'll solve the mystery by pointing to the new employee you hired.

You also set yourself up to become a target if your firm loses *another* account who's a rival of the first. Was the hiring seen as a conflict of interest or a sign of a future favoritism? Perhaps not. But people may be quick to assume the worst.

The bottom line? Take George Washington's advice and stay clear of foreign entanglements.

A CHANCE TO MOVE

1. Outside the Firm: Crossing Industries

As general manager, you may believe (or be persuaded to believe) that a manager's a manager. You may think the skills you've got in industry X apply equally well in industry Y because people are people and products are products. You may assume the know-how you've acquired placing auto batteries in auto and tire shops across the land will serve you well if you're called upon to place computer software in computer stores across the land. Right?

Wrong. The two industries have widely diverse cultures due to difference in products in terms of market volatility and product lifespan. Moving ahead in the culture of one industry may prove an insurmountable hurdle if it's radically different from your own specialty—particularly if you've become well known in the industry where you've established your business identity. If the coat-and-tie image of your tire sales background has rooted itself in your psyche, you may not feel comfortable at board meetings with whiz kids clad in jeans and T-shirts. And if you're uncomfortable, you probably won't perform well. Because the chemistry isn't right, the others, feeling that you don't fit, won't *let* you perform well.

Now, we're not suggesting that you can't make a career change or that the problems of one industry leave you with zero qualifications to enter another, but be warned by the negative experiences of many. Thousands of talented executives have found themselves without portfolio within six months after an unsuccessful attempt to adjust to a new culture in a new industry. Remember, you bring your greatest value in the business area where you bring expertise to the table.

As a senior-level manager, you're being paid a high salary because you're the pro. Your in-depth knowledge about the industry, the products and services makes you worth that salary. Generally speaking, the more able you are to apply extensive knowledge, within relatively narrow industry boundaries, the greater will be your value.

I'd have to say that over the years as many executives have been hurt by change as have made great leaps forward. Witness our previous references to marketing executives moving to banking, or to the Scott Paper training problem.

When industries decide it's time for change, they'll often attempt to transplant or graft culture from another industry they admire. At one time or another, companies like Union Carbide, Monsanto, Mattel, Gillette, Atari, etc., have tried with varying lack of success to have the graft take.

While a company may suffer, the much-publicized executive often departs in a shower of sparks, press releases, and failure.

Many of these executives have an extremely difficult time getting back into other companies. Often they have been enticed away with lucrative compensation packages, including stock, just to *consider* the move. Anything less is looked on as unacceptable even if former industry standards cannot support the giant compensation packages the "glamour" companies can provide.

2. Moving without Portfolio

Another "golden opportunity" that tends to surface about this time in a fast-track career is the "special EVP" position. More typical in smaller companies than huge public corporations, this spot is usually presented to the unwary by top executives who speak in vague but glowing terms of an opportunity to "work closely" at the top and "shape the company to your thinking and experience."

It's also clearly implied that the president is "putting the house in order" with an eye to retiring, and that you, as the right-hand person, will be heir apparent after a suitable grooming period. It seldom happens.

In all my years of counseling executives on various career options, I can count on one hand the number of times the scenario has played out. Some people, like the founder of a leading cosmetics company, are said to have used this technique for over twenty years to woo a steady stream of hopeful executives to their company. Always the great promise, the future of someday running the company, always the same disappointing result.

Breakpoint Forces

The translation of this glittering generality boils down to two most likely occurrences. The first is that the position calls for a hatchet man. The president doesn't want to create an outright rebellion and cloud a corporate image as the paternal goodwill bearer and provider, so you're brought in as the tough act from company X who's gung ho for ruthless cost-cutting policies.

You're in for a period of playing black hat to his white hat. At the end of the firing line, you'll have garnered the resentment of everyone left behind and have the allegiance of none.

Furthermore, once you've set the house in order, the president is likely to conclude that things can run very well without too much strain in the newly organized fashion, and that he or she can put off retirement for another few years.

You, on the other hand, may have outlived your usefulness at this firm and soon be negotiating your severance package from a position of weakness.

Then there is the president who just has to have your great experience and expertise at all costs. The marriage is made and goes smoothly for a few months, at which time one of two things may occur. The most common problem I've seen is a cultural mismatch between the new executive and the management of the new company. With change comes resistance; with resistance comes pressure and resentment. The resentment manifests itself in unhappy working relationships and ultimate separation.

Or the president finds that the new move will cost more than was bargained for. New this, new that, and the frustrated new executive, having to wear many new hats, can't seem to keep fingers on all the buttons, something that was taken for granted at the former company with strong staff support. The result is management disillusion with the new approach.

While many companies come to mind, none is a better example than the old Commodore Company run by Jack Tramiel. According to executives who had departed, he imported talent to run the company, then changed direction often, either firing or driving away the staff when they didn't fit with the new direction.

Breakpoint Strategy

When faced with a "right-hand man" offer, don't bite until you have a firm contract with a generous severance package and don't sign until you have researched and see solid and ongoing operational responsibilities spelled out in the contract.

Even if you like the idea of being the "new broom" charged with cleaning up the act, it may not be an asset on your résumé unless you achieve. If your stay is short-lived, relatively brief tenure will result in a question mark on your record, reflecting at least questions of judgment. Typically, you won't have positive success stories for which you can claim credit, since you won't be staying around long enough to have your achievements come to fruition. Your track record in this job will likely be difficult to describe in a positive manner and may haunt you later.

Move 3: "The Loser and New President . . ."

A variant of the "hatchet" problem is the offer to leapfrog from your general manager's spot to the presidency of (often) a smaller company. This is by far the most common reason for moving. The tempting offer several levels higher. A scenario that presents itself is often an entrepreneurial president who's got the company running profitably and wants you to bring in your big-company stabilizing influence to take the reins for the long haul.

The pitch you'll get is that Mr. Entrepreneur gets great satisfaction solely from starting up companies and breaking new ground, and is looking to you as the keeper of the keys to whom can be entrusted operations while he is summering in Maine, wintering in St. Maarten, and occasionally dabbling in new start-up ideas as inspiration strikes.

A key question to ask here is: "How many other companies have you started up and left management to?" If we're talking about a half dozen or more, you might take what Mr. Entrepreneur says at face value. If the number is any less, you run the risk that the brainchild will never be turned over and that your great contributions will be viewed as intrusion. The entrepreneurial temperament tends not to be the same as that of the up-through-the-ranks manager, and often sparks fly as the operating experience of the latter proves unsatisfactory to the former.

To many an entrepreneurial type, you may also represent everything the entrepreneur tried to escape by forming a new business. And though the entrepreneur proclaims in virtuous tones fidelity to "sound business practices" and "today's M.B.A. techniques," this commitment is likely to be forgotten at the first crisis period.

As you try to apply methods that you've used successfully in the past, you may experience interference followed by more interference, for beneath the surface there's a psychological battle being fought over who's really in charge and whose ego needs massaging.

Don't make the mistake, as many of our high-tech friends have learned, of believing that holding a large block of stock as part of your compensation package will give you any more clout in this situation. Unless everything is agreed upon in advance or the entrepreneur, absolutely desperate for you to join, is willing to turn over majority voting power, you can expect that your effort to bring "M.B.A. management" to the company will get a response similar to what U.S. revenue agents might expect from backwoods distillers.

Move 4: Overseas

At the general manager level, an overseas move usually presents great opportunity. The position you're likely to land can provide complete control and good visibility at the home office; you, if anyone, will get credit for good things that happen.

Since you're at the top of the local pyramid, there's little chance you'll be ignored or that your efforts will be unappreciated. Accordingly, this is the time to take this chance, absent other considerations to the contrary, assuming you have taken time to closely evaluate your career chart.

From a Machiavellian standpoint, the foreign office can present a lesser risk of career-harming failure. Though you're the person at whose desk the buck stops, factors causing foreign disasters are inevitably suitably mysterious and complex to the home office. A sudden downturn in profitability can be attributed to regional causes, especially if you're in hostile territory. In some countries today, one could conceivably make failure seem like success just by meeting the payroll and paying the taxes.

SPECIAL POINTERS

1. At the general manager level, trappings like wardrobe become more expensive and necessary. High-quality, authoritative yet conservative style is significantly overpriced in many areas of the country, but it is a must, for you'll be closely observed from above and below.

   Many people, especially women with families, tend to skimp on this investment—unless there's a bountiful cash flow to draw on—in favor of "more important" expenditures. You feel that your family could vacation in Switzerland or Mexico if you "get by" without spending the extra money. And of course you'd prefer to spend the money on the family rather than your clothier.

   Don't. While you certainly want the family top of mind, you have a basic duty to yourself and to your company to look the part they're paying you to play. If you expect to keep moving up, you've got to fulfill this part of the bargain. In the long run your family will benefit and your promotions will continue.

2. There are few women at the general manager level, and fewer still, relatively speaking, at the officer level. If you're female, you may have no "model" on which to base your dress style. Accordingly, your own taste should prevail. You know the industry you're in and you know the way the men dress. You have "safe" models in Congress and in the White House—or perhaps at 10 Downing Street—but feel free to expand to suit the way your male counterparts expand on "safe" models *they* find in Congress and the White House. Generally speaking, we've found most successful female executives

maintain an image that's conservative, neat, yet forceful—the flowers are on the desk, not in the pattern of their clothes.

3. On the fast track, the general manager level quite likely involves a key move. If you're married, saying "yes" to the move will mean taking your family along. There's no easy way to get through the extremely difficult choice this presents to you and your spouse. Someone has to give. If one person wants to stay, there are bound to be problems or perhaps great expense as long-distance commuting becomes a reality.

Our recommendation is to use your career chart to address this problem in advance. Sit down with your spouse and perhaps your family, although in my experience families are very resistant to moves. Talk over the new position and lay out where you want to go. Let them know where you want to be five years from now, ten years from now, and set down the steps to get there, including geographic changes that may be required. While it may not persuade your spouse to move along with you, getting the discussion out in the open will let you both know where you stand. With proper lead time, the exchange may provide time to think it over, approach the subject less emotionally, and realize how serious you are. Perhaps your spouse will decide to go along if the real opportunity comes. For families without children or without children at home, the choice can be easier, but we've found that there isn't any easy answer.

CHECKLIST FOR SPOUSES

1. In the main portion of this chapter, we've pointed out to your working spouse the need to think defensively about certain projects at work. It's likely that some of this controlled paranoia, fussing, and moaning will find its way home at the end of the day, and that you'll be greeted by a spouse who's not eager to hear your plans for the evening.

It's up to you to assert yourself and not let negative thinking get out of hand. We don't recommend that you make a mechanical effort to quash all less than positive thoughts about work when your spouse is home. But we do want to emphasize that a break from the workplace is necessary, and that your spouse ought to know this by now. Sometimes a reminder that a break is overdue will help.

2. On the fast track, conspicuous consumption is an occupational disease. To show upward mobility and mingle with the "right set," too many have spent far too much for too little over too short a time, with too great a number of installment-loan payments.

   You can help avoid unnecessarily painful money pressures by not taking your role too seriously. Of course, *some* keeping up with your peers is necessary, but it should not be exaggerated. Try to distance yourself from business displays that are required. Especially avoid thinking that your spouse's promotion is like a dukedom, carrying with it certain entitlements. This fantasy is present too frequently to shore up sagging social confidence—and it's a rubber crutch. If your sense of self-worth is dependent upon fantasies about your spouse's job, you'll have difficulty objectively assisting in real career decisions for the future.

   If you happen to be among the fortunate few who have two powerful incomes, try to avoid an excessive display of your good fortune to your spouse's work colleagues. A wife's jealous colleagues may surmise that she doesn't need the money and is just doing the job as a hobby and probably should be taken less seriously. As for the husband of this couple, jealous tongues have been known to wag that he has married a rich woman and wouldn't be in this position were it not for her money. In either case, the display hurts one or the other spouse.

3. When the inevitable "required" move comes along, priorities will obviously color your career choices. You may ask: Is it more important for your spouse to keep moving up the career ladder, or is it more important to stay in this nice community where you've both been happy and where the children are doing so well?

   The choice can seem simple and your spouse's career drive may appear to be no more than ambition. However, as executives worldwide have experienced the fast track, a "required" move means what it says. To say "no" to the move may also be saying "no" to life in a similar happy environment, since the job market probably won't provide the same income stream for an executive who isn't willing to follow company orders (or requests, if you prefer).

Tolerance, foresight, and your assessment of the risks involved should form the basis of discussions with your spouse when evaluating each move. At this level in particular, you should be clear what the stakes are and how much is at risk. Discuss the stakes and project forward all possible ramifications.

A special problem arises when both spouses are fast-track and both face "required" moves that will take them in opposite directions. In the stress created by this infrequent but extremely painful event, people we know have used various methods to resolve the conflict. We've seen coins flipped, straws drawn, and we've seen temporary separations. The method that seems most equitable is the one that we think works *least* effectively, but we mention it here: the "trade-off" or "take turns" solution. Spouse A gets to move the family the first time, and the other spouse takes what is available in the new location. When spouse B gets to a breakpoint and a required move, spouse A has to tag along. What this does, in our experience, is create two would-be fast-track candidates, neither of whom can fulfill the obligations that go with being on the fast track. It makes decisions about the career a "your turn—my turn" scenario rather than a well-thought-through plan dealing with logical criteria for decisions in each case.

A better solution from a career standpoint may be to agree in advance which spouse will stay on the fast track and which spouse will follow. In so doing, each party knows where he/she stands, and career plans aren't thwarted each time a new opportunity presents itself.

Chapter 13

Officer
Steady Path

Capsule Summary

Your job as corporate officer may be worlds apart from that of another corporate officer of the identical rank. So, depending on your duties and responsibilities, the breakpoints you encounter may bear more resemblance to those we've described in the chapters about the general manager; if you're with a *very* small company, the breakpoints you encounter may more closely resemble those we describe for the entrepreneur.

For now, though, let's assume that your position is with a medium-sized or larger company, and that your primary concerns about production and motivation will closely resemble those of the general manager, entrepreneur, and CEO. We recommend that you review those chapters as part of your career evaluation exercise.

The reality of officer-level operations is that your routine may shift from production to policy. Once cloaked with the mantle of "EVP" or "comptroller," you may be forced to become a public affairs-minded, politically sensitive "business community leader."

Regrettably, if you set out to live the image, you'll probably wind up only half an officer—and a temporary half at that. I've known officers who devoted so much time to outside pursuits that they lost control of their companies and their lives.

On the other side of the coin, one top executive spent so much time fund raising that when fired from his job he became a professional nonprofit fund raiser. The responsibility had given him the opportunity to see a new career choice and he took it.

Whether on the steady path or the fast track, your concern must be for the bottom line. Resist temptation to let the role of "business community leader" turn you into a politician, philosopher, or philanthropist, unless, of course, this is an objective.

On the personal level, beware of the pressures of a public image. The fishbowl existence is a familiar hazard, and the stress it places on you and your family can accelerate pace and tension.

In the political realm at work, you'll still have the familiar presence from above from the CEO—but there will seldom be the "mentor" relationship you may have enjoyed with your previous bosses. Instead, there may be competition and dissension. Concerns that seemed trivial in earlier career stages are magnified by their symbolic importance. There may be attempts to involve you in a "palace revolt," or at least to use your influence to sway an issue in favor of another executive. Navigating these political shoals can be uncertain at best, with development of outside contacts—and a strong contract—more essential than ever.

PERFORMANCE BREAKPOINTS

Some companies have four officers. Some companies have fifty. If you're an executive vice-president, your duties can be absolutely essential to the company, or absolutely not. Variations in titles at the officer level occasionally do credit to the creativity of the human spirit. "Executive vice-president—coordination." "Senior executive vice-president—management innovation." "Junior executive vice-president for interdepartmental activities." These titles offer few clues to the demands and responsibility of the job. They're all real titles, but the duties involved are shrouded in mystery.

Yet one universal trait connects these three: they're all "officers." This means that the company's list of officers available to the public will include them—and you, if you're among them.

So as an officer you're in the limelight, albeit perhaps amorphous. How you handle this role may determine your tenure in the executive suite.

Breakpoint Signals

Phone calls started coming the first day Irv moved into his top-floor office. Fresh from a successful stint as general manager of an overseas branch, Irv was delighted to be back in the States and eager to implement the production changes he'd learned from the Japanese.

With an eye on this priority, his first executive act was to dictate a list of people within the company whose calls should be put through immediately. His secretary was given his old Rolodex and instructed to put through any caller who was on the "priority" cards. All others were to be asked for messages and numbers taken for callbacks.

The first few days, it seemed as though Irv was on the phone constantly. The public relations firm had successfully placed Irv's picture and brief biography in many trade and business publications and newspapers, and this was the late 1970s, when Japanese production was a hot topic. Congratulatory and welcome-back calls poured in.

When he wasn't on the phone, get-acquainted meetings with home office committees took up what Irv thought was a ridiculous amount of time. The few free hours he had were filled with new organizational routine-setting paperwork, and some precious planning time devoted to his new production project. He worked hard on both phases, knowing the importance of a good start in a new post.

By the end of the third day—just when he was starting to feel as if the job might be manageable after all—his secretary put through a call from the vice-president for operations—Irv's immediate superior. It seemed that the VP's wife belonged to a business club which had a fund-raising dinner coming up. The topic was to be our country's business relations with Japan. Guess whom she wanted to come to dinner. "Sue says she's been trying for two days to get through to you, but that you aren't returning calls. Better watch that kind of thing. We've a responsibility to the community, you know."

Irv got the message, and with sinking heart he examined the stack of "while you were out" slips that had accumulated during his first three days on the job. Nearly a third of them were from similar organizations.

Dutifully, Irv set about returning the calls.

His speech for Sue's club was a hit. Irv had always been a bit of a ham, and his years in the Orient had given him some fine stories. He left the lectern to warm applause and later was commended by the CEO himself —whose wife had been in the audience.

After two or three more speeches, Irv got another call from the VP. "A little change in Irv's assignment." To capitalize on the exposure opportunity, Irv now had a schedule of events to attend as company representative. As a result of his "new assignment," Irv carried his company's banner in the cause of American-Japanese business relations across the country for nearly two years.

Of course, his pet production project was shelved—then taken over by another EVP. When the enchantment with Japanese methods wore off, Irv found himself with fewer invitations and smaller audiences. His office on the top floor wasn't buzzing with phone calls anymore. When he went to the VP to ask for another assignment, he was told that the company didn't have one for him "at this time." He wasn't to get a raise that year, either.

"I'd lost my base," Irv recalls now. "It was as though all those previous years doing real work didn't count. I'd become some kind of entertainer— some kind of fad—and I was out of fashion. Hard to believe."

Fortunately, during his travels Irv had accumulated thousands of contacts—in fact, one of the most impressive networks we've ever seen. When he came to us, we were able to construct a plan to assist him to locate a production position that would let him draw on his "hard" knowledge. Within three months, he was number-two man at a smaller company, and when we last heard from him, he'd risen to number one. "I still make some speeches from time to time," he tells us, "but I'm a production guy, not a PR professional any longer."

Breakpoint Forces

Public relations is a major part of every corporate officer's job description—whether it's performed or not. With heavily leveraged financing more the rule than the exception, privately held corporations are as conscious of public opinion as the publicly held corporations who rely on the market to raise capital. They know that the lending officers who hold the keys to the coffers are swayed by the public perception of the company, regardless of their concern for the company's balance sheet.

Good financial projections alone just won't compete with a borrowing proposal whose numbers are equally good but the mention of whose company name draws nods of respectful recognition at the loan committee meetings. Regulators, too, are swayed by a strong company image. The same is true for employees, who get a boost in morale when their families and friends are impressed by favorable company publicity.

The net result is that PR is a game everyone at the officer level must play. It requires a good deal of work, but it can be a fun game as well. Public service is good for the soul and applause is good for the ego.

The key is knowing how to modulate for maximum success with minimal downside.

Breakpoint Strategy

If you are not careful, playing the public relations game can distract you from the simple truth that corporations are in business to make a profit for the shareholders. While PR may be the major role for the president, your power base in the company relates to the performance of your division— the products or services it provides for the company. On any given day, hundreds of "important" opportunities to influence public opinion can come your way. Try to handle them whenever appropriate, but do not let them distract you from the bottom line.

Irv let himself be railroaded into taking what amounted to a two-year leave of absence. His power base withered. Don't let your need to fulfill your newly acquired PR duties or any other staff function lead you down the garden path away from your power base.

Before you mount a lectern or agree to an interview, take time to prepare yourself to do the job well. Get a good grounding from your corporate legal department on potential liabilities in your talk and liability issues. Check current securities and tax issues. Aside from the company's intention to build new factories or cut pollution, these are the topics you're most likely to be queried about on the corporate platform. It's a good idea to be familiar with current issues in worldwide areas as well, whether or not your company is involved in international trade. A quick and assured reply when asked about the balance of payments or trade protectionism scores points; an uncertain look or hesitancy labels your company as at least unprepared.

PERSONAL BREAKPOINTS: "THE GOLDFISH BOWL"

You've been warned, of course. For generations, movies and novels—not to mention daytime TV—have gleefully dissected the strains of life at the top on the psyches of executives' wives and children. The patterns are familiar. A wife cracks under the strain of too many lonely nights, too many unaccepted dinner invitations, or too few votes for her at the garden club election. The kids take to drugs and drink at the country club. They're seething inwardly because Dad didn't play catch or jacks with them during their formative years, and they know that public misbehaving is a great way to get revenge by embarrassing him.

There's often a crash toward the end of the tale—usually in a new and very expensive car. Tears and accusations follow. The gist of the accusations is that Dad loves his job more than his family. Hurt and defensive, Dad retorts that he's misunderstood and that no one appreciates all the sacrifices he made to put the family where it is. Behind the interpersonal drama there's the not too subtle hint that the real villain is the family's social-climbing aspiration, and that they'd have been better off had they stayed "in their place," European style. While it does occur in real life and we all know several examples, success at work doesn't doom families. There is evidence that top executives who did not communicate with their children would not have communicated if they were at lower levels either. Also, not too long ago, the children of successful senior executives were polled and the response was overwhelmingly supportive of the lifestyle and relationship with parents. In fact, as a group, these children were among the happiest in the nation.

So in real life there are large numbers of families where the breadwinner is a top-level executive and the spouse and kids are socially confident.

Breakpoint Forces

What distinguishes happy families from the unhappy ones? Judging from our experience at G&S, we find there are three major differences.

One. They have strong social graces; because they've had the good fortune to be born into a family of upper-level means or because they've taken the time to work at it, they treat each other well.

Two. They understand social traditions that accompany a position of leadership—their European roots and the noblesse oblige tradition—and they don't take them too seriously.

Three. They view extra activities as part of the job. Particularly if they're a first-generation family in the upper level, they view what they are doing as part of what comes with the territory. They do not attempt to create an illusion that they've always had wealth, or that they're entitled to a papal audience or a trip to the White House simply because Dad or Mom has been promoted. The need to join the "right" club or attend the "right" schools and social events is simply one of the trade-offs for the freedom to do things that the increased salary makes possible.

Breakpoint Strategy

How do you engender this attitude in your family? The first step is to have this attitude as part of your own makeup. You won't be convincing if secretly you yearn to be as regal as many of your top management counterparts may seem.

If you're in a company of any significant size, it's unlikely that you've come this far without "social graces." Since the majority of companies also screen families, it's unlikely that your loved ones will need much "polishing." But if they do, see that the appropriate lessons are learned—and avoid making a major production out of the experience. Some parents imply that the family home will be lost if daughter doesn't know which fork to use, creating misplaced emotional intensity—no matter how unfairly critical the prying eyes of other top-level executives or their spouses may be.

POLITICAL BREAKPOINTS: "COMES THE REVOLUTION"

Stewart worked as production EVP for a medium-sized textile-manufacturing company in North Carolina. The firm was doing well, with a hundred and fifty employees on the payroll and new orders running nine months ahead of production. Stewart's only problem area was the president's style of management. A former army colonel, the CEO ran the company along military lines, on a "need to know" basis. The secretive, rigid, authoritarian command structure was inappropriate, Stewart thought, for such a small company, but he had been on board for ten years and had learned the ways of the chief. He thought he'd adapted rather well and was reasonably content with things as they were.

Then late one afternoon, Mark, the EVP in charge of sales, stopped Stewart in the parking lot. After a hesitant look around as if to make sure they weren't being watched from afar, Mark said, "A group of us are stopping by my house tonight to talk over the situation. We'd like to have you with us."

"What situation?" Stewart wanted to know. Mark looked at him quietly for a moment, and then let his eyes flicker back to the top floor of the plant, where the CEO's light still burned. "The old man," he said. "We think he's standing in the way of what this company could really achieve, and I know at least two of the directors who feel the same way."

Reluctantly, Stewart had to admit he agreed, and that evening he found himself joining with the others in the group—the third EVP, the treasurer, and two of the directors—in preparing a memorandum to the board. The language of the memo was very restrained and no mention was made of the CEO, only of policies made and opportunities missed. The message, however, was clear.

There were two meetings of the board of directors following that evening's gathering. At the first, the memorandum was presented. At the second, the majority of the board of directors voiced their confidence in the CEO and offered the three EVPs the opportunity to resign or be dismissed. Stunned, Stewart found himself looking for work at age fifty-six, with a minimal severance package and a wife who'd already picked out their retirement home.

We were fortunate in helping him relocate—his experience and track record were very impressive. But the upheaval of moving was traumatic. To make matters worse, Stewart later found out that one of the two "revolutionary" directors had been in league with the CEO from the beginning. "The whole pitiful mess was the CEO's doing," Stewart recounts. "He sensed some disloyalty and used one of his director cronies to smoke it out. He sure as hell succeeded."

Breakpoint Forces

As a steady-path officer, you are on the political fence, and a potential ally for whatever side is anxious to take control in a palace revolt. Such revolts are more likely to fail than to succeed. If the CEO is weak enough to be in need of overthrowing, the directors probably are already aware of the situation—or can be made aware on a discreetly informal basis rather than through anything as risky as a direct challenge.

Breakpoint Strategy

When it appears that a rebellion is brewing, try to recognize that there's no sure way to protect your position. Whether you take sides or remain neutral, there's no guarantee that the eventual winner will not want to replace you. If you come out on the losing side, as Stewart did, you are, of course, sure to be among the departed in short order. Even if you support the winner, there may be a desire to bring in a new team and you will find yourself replaced.

The obvious strategy, then, when your company is about to become embroiled in a king-of-the-hill dispute, is to activate your contacts and look for a new backup position outside the company. Since this takes some time, don't procrastinate. You may be pleased you took some action.

SPECIAL POINTERS

Such a small percentage of women in business achieve officer level that the temptation for a woman to overindulge in her public relations role may be intensified by strong media interest. Women executives are hot news and reporters seek them out. In addition to consuming your time, the media can distort your message. The reporter invariably wants a version of a "how I made it to the top as a woman" story, complete with fan-magazine-type questions about sacrificed romance, unattended children, and attention-starved spouse.

It can be disconcerting to grant an interview on world economic policies as they relate to your company's future expansion goals only to find that the discussion has been turned into a human-interest story in the Sunday-supplement family pages. This kind of story doesn't help either you or your company as much as the story you intended to give. To avoid it, either rule out or screen closely human-interest interviews—and questions—at your initial meeting with the reporter. I recall clearly a speech given by Mary Cunningham a year or two ago which she began by stating what she was *not* going to talk about. A good strategy.

CHECKLIST FOR SPOUSES

As the spouse of an officer, you may find yourself either loving or hating the increased time spent in PR activity. You may enjoy sharing the limelight. You may find that you've got a welcome opportunity to influence what your spouse says in public and to feel proud of being an advisory force behind the scenes.

On the other hand, you may see the increased "public life" as another trial that your spouse has to go through, and fall back on your past long-suffering patience, telling yourself not to interfere.

If taken to excess, either of these two approaches—the enthusiastic supporter or the overly passive observer—can do your spouse a disservice. As we point out in the central portion of the text in this chapter, exaggerated PR emphasis can undermine your spouse's strength at work and can lead to future assignments that are less than satisfying. You should keep a weather eye out for excessive PR and mention to your spouse when you feel that he or she's neglecting the base required to remain viable at work.

Chapter 14

Officer
Fast Track

Capsule Summary
The performance breakpoints for a fast-track officer include those we've
set forth for the general manager and steady-path officer—not to mention
those we've discussed in earlier chapters. The special problem for a fast-
track officer is that the pyramid suddenly narrows dramatically at the top.
General rule: For you to move up, someone above you must move—and
there's usually no room for that someone to move up. This final step
creates the most difficult and sensitive personnel infighting in the workplace.

PERFORMANCE BREAKPOINTS

At the officer level on the fast track, the difference between moving up
and moving out is more dependent on your political skills and relationships than virtually anything else. Put another way, at this level, your work
performance *is* your political performance. You're motivating subordinates
with more than managerial skills, since you've gone far beyond the level at
which actual production, sales, and training work is accomplished.

Accordingly, the important things you do become the important people
you know. Your job becomes one of setting policy and using your contacts
to orchestrate a team effort that's far more inclusive and far more subtle
than just working hard to turn out a crash project. Your overall focus is

broad—reviewing your company's position in the industry rather than the specific tasks that will give the company its position.

A number of years ago the president of a major U.S. consumer goods conglomerate told me that his greatest concern when bringing an executive along in the company was to get a handle on whether the individual could gradually move from a "hands on" mentality to one where policy and broad overview were a prime focus.

He called this transition "management menopause" and claimed that it was a rare talent for an individual who could perform well in both areas to be able to make the switch effortlessly.

At the time I questioned both the rarity and the relative difficulty he described. But as with many other firm business conclusions I developed in early years, today I'm certain he was right. In fact, I'd zero in more specifically and say that after meeting hundreds of senior executives all driven toward the same goal, the most important style issue at the senior levels becomes visionary—evaluating and keeping the big picture in mind while shifting management roles to delegate through the organization.

Breakpoint Signals: "A Tiger by the Tail"

You've enough "on the plate" in your division for fifty officers, it seems. You have a challenging and important role—as we've pointed out, it is key to the company's success.

But your time isn't your own. You get the feeling that there's too much detail to this job for you and that there's no way you can conquer each of the myriad problems that cross your desk without devoting your fullest energies to the task.

Breakpoint Forces

If you give in to this "job-consuming" mentality, you'll have reached your plateau, and your chances for movement to a CEO spot are greatly reduced. Even if sparkling performance in your particular division gets you an offer or two in an outside company, you won't have picked up the key delegatory skills and contacts that you need to manage the CEO job.

As a result, you'd be an on-the-job trainee in the CEO spot. Few boards will hire you and fewer still will want to retain you under those conditions.

Breakpoint Strategy

Delegate, delegate, delegate. You *must* compress the duties in your division so they take up no more than 75 percent of your work time. The remaining 25 percent should be spent on matters important to your company's *overall* future.

If your division is key to the company's success, you can use the obvious need to relate better with other company functions to justify the 25 percent in these "outside" areas.

Just as important, take part of your 25 percent and use it to develop your contacts throughout the industry.

Again, the need for your department or division to interrelate with other parts of the company is your primary justification. You need to see how other outfits are operating; you need to see what recommendations suppliers, regulators, and vendors have for your division based on their experience with other companies in the field.

Of course, what you are doing is building a network of contacts that will lead you to CEO opportunities in other companies. You'll also build the contacts you'd need in the event your own CEO were to step down and you were asked to step up.

How do you compress what's overwhelming you now into 75 percent of your work time? You spend more time interviewing and screening for aggressive, eager, and efficient subordinates who are ready, willing, and able to take up your work load. You terminate—or commit to early retirement—those who don't. You then devote a sizable chunk of that 75 percent to keeping your productive subordinates happy—by lobbying for the raises to keep them motivated, as well as creating other incentives they need to retain their productivity.

PERSONAL BREAKPOINTS

Breakpoint Signals

Things weren't well at the midwestern manufacturing company where Brian was comptroller. The overexpansive policies of the "bullish" CEO had taken the company too far too fast. Debt structure had begun to eat up the once-attractive bottom-line profits, and the earnings per share were less than when the charismatic CEO had taken over with his vision of tripling the company's output within as many years. It took Brian's best resources to ensure that each month's payroll would be met—not only in refinancing but in maximizing the cash-flow potential. "I had some real arm-twisting sessions with our lenders," Brian recalls. "There were times when I wondered why I was selling the company rather than the CEO, but that was my job—to see that our financing stayed in place."

One week after the quarterly report went to the board, Brian received a call from one of the directors. The call didn't seem business-related—it came in the form of an invitation to the director's golf club. "He said they were expanding their membership and he thought I might drop by if I was interested," Brian said.

On the links, the director was carefully neutral about any company-related conversations. He said that he was interested in the president's plans and that he thought some of the goals the new company had in mind would be a credit to the industry. Without going beyond these innocuous and offhand remarks, he concluded the round with Brian and suggested they drop by the clubhouse for a drink.

In the clubhouse bar, the director became a bit more expansive, and the questions began. Each was phrased, Brian now recalls, in a 100 percent loyal manner that didn't imply any criticism of the CEO. The projected earnings from the newly acquired subsidiary: they'd generate a more than adequate return after debt service, wouldn't they? The projected orders for the new product line: those would more than cover the additional capital required for production, right? "At the back of my mind, I thought something was up," Brian remembers. "But I didn't want to face up to my suspicions that the director was testing the president's assumptions. Instead, I thought he was testing *me*."

Rather than give his frank appraisal of the bullish assumptions that the CEO's plans all hinged on, Brian hedged. "I came on like a good, solid team player," he says now with more than a little chagrin. "I didn't mention my hunch that the projected interest rates for debt structure were on the wrong trend. Nor did I go into the studies our department had done in forecasting the sales potential versus production expenses during the next few years. Our forecasts had been conveniently ignored by the CEO in favor of more optimistic reports published in recent national media. I could have given the director a real earful. If I'd been honest, I'd have told him what I thought of the CEO's blind optimism and reckless spending. I'd also have mentioned a few other areas in the company where I'd try to offset his incompetent decisions.

"Imagine my surprise a month later when I learned that the board had been considering me as a possible replacement for the CEO. I learned this from one of my banker friends—the morning after the board replaced the CEO with a man of my own background. My banker friend couldn't understand why the board hadn't chosen to promote from within. I knew. I learned the hard way."

Breakpoint Forces

Those with the "killer instinct" don't have the problem Brian had. After a career spent being loyal to those above him, Brian didn't allow himself to break free of past conditioning and tell it "like it was." At the level of director versus CEO, loyalty has to take second priority to getting full and accurate information. When there's a problem, it can't be hidden —or the company will suffer.

Don't allow feelings of loyalty to be disturbed by feelings of guilt, Macbeth style. Your CEO isn't a CEO by divine right; this person is leading the company because performance justifies it. The lives of those below— including yours and your family's—are affected by the decisions that keep him or her in power. You owe it to yourself, your family, and everyone else in the company not to cover up what could result in harm—even if you aren't eager to take over the corner office just yet. Remember, you can discuss issues without making them black or white by addressing alternatives. In this way, you can present data and show others that, while not being disloyal, you can think issues through on several levels.

Breakpoint Strategy

If you let your feelings of loyalty to the person above you override the need to be accurate about company problems, you will stay in a number-two spot. If you know of problems the way Brian did, take the opportunities you get to offer solutions at appropriate levels.

The Macbeth guilt syndrome is a trap that lurks most frequently at this level, since to get to the top position, often the "king" has to be "killed." Unless there's a move to head up another company, a company CEO doesn't get promoted, unlike other bosses you've worked under. If you let the sadness a departing CEO will feel at being "kicked upstairs" or being forced to take early retirement affect your judgment, you've sabotaged your own career. Not to mention the future of the company, if indeed you were the one to lead it.

Keep your eye on career opportunities and take heed on those occasions when the chips *should* fall where they may.

POLITICAL BREAKPOINTS

Breakpoint Signals

In a well-ordered company, the chance to move up to the CEO spot generally appears well in advance of the actual transition. The CEO will be looking to retirement—either at a voluntary date or at the company's mandatory age. Assuming that the company is stable, the CEO's natural wish to appoint a successor will find favor with the directors, since presumably they're pleased with the CEO's performance and eager for stability and continuity.

A clear signal that you may be in the running occurs when the CEO's retirement plans are made known and no new person is brought on board at an EVP level to be "groomed." If it's clear that the successor will come "from the ranks," the CEO will probably make preferences known in advance. You'll know one way or the other if you're among the top two or three to be considered—you may even learn this from a newspaper article.

If you find yourself in one of these "healthy competition" contests, you have two choices: either play the game or throw your support to one of the other candidates. In either case, the situation calls for backup measures—since, assuming you want a CEO spot, you'll have a long wait if you come out in second or third place. If you've entered the race at full speed and wind up in second or third place, of course, you can count on a short time to wait before being eased out by your victorious competitor.

In the event you're playing the game, you will need absolute discretion in pursuing backup plans. The hint that you're looking elsewhere can easily be used against you and scotch your chances. Conversely, the appearance that you're turning away eager suitors can add to your prestige and desirability.

In any event, to win the race for the top spot, one question we find useful to ask is: "What are the current CEO's chief constituencies within the company?" The odds are, assuming that the company is stable, that the CEO has support from the "grass roots" on up. In the political melee of a three-way run for the roses, many competitors are prone to focus on the decision makers—the CEO and the board—as well as their peers at the officer level from whom they need cooperation for day-to-day performance. They ignore the grass-roots constituencies within the company.

Breakpoint Strategy

As we've mentioned earlier, the three most important performance strategies for the fast-track officer are to delegate, to delegate, and to delegate. The same advice holds true for at-work political activities. Free your time to widen your political base within the company. Use the opportunities that company-wide activity and informal management contacts give you to create support at all levels of the company. It becomes obvious to a CEO when an immediate subordinate has a strong following—and if you're in the running for the CEO stamp of approval as replacement, you have license to go out and campaign. Ideally, you'll have been "out there" on a regular basis from the beginning of your stay with the company, and you'll already have favorite-son or -daughter status.

SPECIAL POINTERS

At the officer level, you'll have many executive subordinates. If you're a woman, you may find yourself being harder on those subordinates who happen to be female. Beware of this attitude.

The reasons for your "tougher" attitude may be complex and may even seem necessary to you. You believe that it's important for women to move up and that you're doing other women a service by ensuring that only the best move up. You may feel that "riding" a female subordinate is good training and discipline for her. You may feel a sense of justice at not letting the female subordinate move up without having her undergo the same trials you went through. You may want to protect yourself from suspicion among your male counterparts that you're "soft on women." Alternatively, you may recognize that your company has room for only one woman at the top, and you may want to keep potential competitors away from your territory.

Whatever your reason, you should stop. Other peers will be quick to see unfairness of this kind, and their reactions won't help your advancement path toward a CEO spot.

CHECKLIST FOR SPOUSES

Other than the terminal phases, the fast-track officer career stage probably presents more stress to a spouse than any other. The goal of CEO is so near and yet so far. So many years have been sacrificed. So much seems to be riding on every little move, it's like the closing minutes of a tie game when victory hangs in the balance. As a "team player," the spouse suffers equally with the fast-track mate. As a parent, the spouse can feel responsible for holding up the entire non-work end of things to leave the fast-track candidate free to pursue an ultimate corner-office goal.

The result of this kind of pressure is often devastating, particularly in the standard situation where the husband's ambition becomes the family's number-one goal. Not only is responsibility for the kids being wrongfully heaped on the wife, but also too much may be made of the family's duty to propel Dad to the top. Kids get the message that disaster will strike if they don't conduct themselves like young princes and princesses and they resent it. Their resentment takes the form, as we've discussed, so well known to psychiatrists and soap-opera fans. Mom, too, is more likely than not to feel overburdened—as well as used.

"But it's the goal that counts," you might think. "It's such a great thing to strive for, we can't be halfhearted." We disagree. Though not taking halfway measures sounds reasonable—even necessary—the attitude expressed here applies to a game, where there is one opponent and on a given day there's always the chance for your team to come out on top. By contrast, the race for a CEO spot isn't held every week during a given season every year. The race for a CEO spot comes around in a given company on average no more than every three to five years, and company officers change jobs even less frequently. The rules of the CEO game aren't printed in a book or enforced by a referee. Forces beyond your control are likely to determine the outcome of the contest and there can be only one winner.

So to pressure your family into feeling as though they're in an all-important race is to set them up for almost certain disappointment—as well as frustration and resentment. Sure, you can point to CEO families who say they were part of the competitive struggle all the way, and to

CEOs who say that family support really made the difference. But don't try to convert this kind of public relations magnanimity into a game plan that you impose on your loved ones. The odds are against you, and if you fail to get the CEO nod, you will not only have lost the opportunity at work, you may have lost vital family support somewhere along the way.

Chapter 15

The Entrepreneur
Instant Chief Executive

Capsule Summary

At any time on your career path, you've got an option to become Mr. President of your own business. As long as you've got $150 or so for corporate state filing fees, a typewriter and stationery to complete the legal forms, and a few dollars extra for a corporate seal (if your state requires one), you can launch your own closely held corporation, assuming you have the capital (usually $1,000) that your state requires to get started. Or, if you're not concerned about insulating yourself from personal liability in your new business, you can begin as a sole proprietor or join forces with a partner.

In today's American business climate, you'll have plenty of company if you take this route. Each business day, 2,200 new businesses are formed. That's 600,000 per year. In some industries—computer software the most publicized—you can be in a basement one year and at the helm of a multimillion-dollar outfit the next, ready to triple your profits for the coming year. It's happened often: we've seen the Apple computer grow from an idea. The media are quick to respond, as are office-supply vendors and advertisers solicitous of the needs of small business. Thus you'll have plenty of glossy in-print encouragement to take the plunge into self-employment.

Sociologists and economists tell us that the trend isn't just a passing fad; that tomorrow's service-oriented economy will use tomorrow's high-tech communications and information-storage capabilities to make one- or two-person offices at home ordinary in the course of doing business for still more Americans.

As if that weren't enough to spur you into the corporate mode, today's tax laws allow significant leeway in retirement and other financial planning if you've got control of ownership to take advantage.

At G&S, we've assisted a number of new entrepreneurs as clients and we've grown to appreciate the viability of this career alternative, particularly for senior-level executives with some available capital.

However, before we present advice on how to make a go of entrepreneurship, we want to point out what we consider the most significant drawbacks:

1. 20 percent of new businesses formed each year fail due to lack of capital.

2. It's not easy to go back to a "mainstream" corporate post after you've been viewed as having bailed out.

Even though you may tire quickly of the unfettered independence associated with self-government, the corporate recruiter isn't likely to be readily convinced. Once you've left the discipline of the "mainstream" workday environment, there is perhaps a risk that you'll do it again and again, as well as judgment issues relating to why you bailed out the first time. The prospect of saying goodbye to you after you've performed up to your glittering potential and made yourself indispensable naturally does not appeal to a prospective employer.

Further, corporate recruiters are not impressed by the often awesome accomplishments you as an entrepreneur have chalked up while learning to "do it all." You may imagine that such achievements give you a most desirable perspective on the true state of business in America, but the reality is that few in corporate circles share this view or admit to it when hiring.

Accordingly, it's tough to go back and even tougher if you've sunk your personal capital into the venture and watched it disappear.

Reentry Mistake: If things are economically tight, you may be tempted to take a job one or two levels below the mainstream spot you left when you struck out on your own. If at all possible, avoid this drop. Take more time to search for a "lateral" move from the mainstream spot you once held; interviewing for a lower position, you'll put yourself at a disadvantage. Either the hiring company will be suspicious about the hidden skeletons that may be prompting you to take a demotion, or, worse, they may exploit what they see as a weakness and use you as a wage slave without seeing you as someone with a future at their company. In either case, the job you'll have won't be much more than a paycheck, and may prove to be only a temporary paycheck while you search elsewhere.

In the event that you do accept a drop in rank, don't be afraid to refer to your past experiences and decisions you made when you occupied your current boss's (or his superior's) post at your old company. You'll make such references with a tactful nod to "changed circumstances" and "new faces," but make them nonetheless. Your contribution will be greater and to abstain is to imply that you were so abysmally wrong in your own experiences that you are afraid even to make reference to them, or that you have burned out, with no interest or ambition to ever reach your former level again.

Temper your experience-based remarks with due deference to your superiors, however. If you leave out the "new circumstances" reference and simply state the way you handled the situation, you'll be directly challenging the authority of your superiors. You'll also be providing the perfect rationale for dismissing your ideas: the implication that your thinking is rooted in the past.

PERFORMANCE BREAKPOINTS

Money, money, money, the three most prominent performance problems of any new business. You've a dream and a good idea, we assume, or you wouldn't be entrepreneuring. But what you don't have is cash. And even your all-purpose entrepreneurial abilities don't include printing the green paper.

Accordingly, the best entrepreneurs we know have paid their dues to their bankers.

Breakpoint Signals

You're in trouble if you think "adversary" when you think of your banker, or if you treasure the feeling of independence from anyone "second-guessing" your newly acquired status as sole authority.

Breakpoint Forces

Sure, you're going to make it big, have cash pouring in on schedule, pay back the original start-up loans, and eventually either sell off with a capital-gains killing or just retire on the income stream. That's the dream that got you hooked.

But if things don't go according to plan, you'll be far from a solution if you haven't prepared the way for adjustments in your credit structure. Though bankers can be understanding, few are eager to step into a workout loan with a stranger. With 20 percent of newly formed businesses folding, the odds are your bank has as many friends who need workout loans as they have workout-loan funds available. The time to look for money is when it is not needed.

Breakpoint Strategy

Here are recommendations for separating yourself from strangers who deal with your bank only on "business" terms.

1. Include your bankers in. Bankers hate to ask for reports more than once. Better to deluge your bankers with spread sheets, charts, and graphs on a monthly basis (after all, they may have loaned you the money to buy the computer that makes these reports almost effortless).

    If your bankers see the inner workings of your company from month to month, they may not make suggestions to help. But if things go wrong and a workout seems required, it will come as no surprise, and they'll be in the position of teammate rather than judge and jury, having been kept in the picture all along.

    Generally it is wise not to limit your reports to those asked for by the bank. Find out what upcoming analyses will be done on your numbers and perform those analyses yourself so that your reports send meaningful signals when they first arrive. If your banker is later forced to choose between a customer whose reports require extra work and yours, guess whom he's likely to favor?

    Also, take advantage of your bank's position in the business community by consulting frequently on the creditworthiness or business reputation of those you deal with. The more you apply to the bank for advice on your business, the more obligated your banker becomes to seeing that the "joint venture" comes out in the black.

2. Include yourself in. Would you be more likely to extend credit to a customer if the customer owned stock in your company? If the customer knew your family, asked about your kids' schools or your wife's or husband's work or club activities? If the customer was a member of your church? If the customer now and again asked you out for a leisurely non-business golf outing or lunch? If your customer knew some of the daily politics within your organization and asked sympathetic or thought-provoking questions about how you were faring in the daily work comedy? If your customer, assuming you were in a corporate structure, asked if you could continue handling the account when you got promoted? If your customer was a friend of your immediate superior? Suggested ways that his expertise could be used?

You can do all this for your banker, of course. In the unlikely event that such advances on your part aren't appreciated, consider changing banks. Create a bond, a solid working relationship during the good times that will survive the bad—and give your banker a record on which to justify increasing your credit when you ask for expansion funding.

PERSONAL BREAKPOINTS

Entrepreneurs consider themselves a pretty special bunch, we have found. This sense of uniqueness can keep them on the move and fuel high energies. On the other hand, it can also create as many "lows" as "highs." The lows generally come when the sense of specialness takes the following forms.

Breakpoint Signal 1

You find yourself believing: "I'm on my own now. I've got to put 100 percent into the effort. No more of this nine-to-five business."

Breakpoint Forces

By defining yourself as your work, you are attempting a change in fundamental human nature. While you may be special, you're still human. You'll be quick to point out that all work and no play makes Jack etc. But the truth of the matter, from our experience, is that eventually either Jack learns to take time off and develop capabilities outside the workplace or he ceases to attract the interest of those who can help move him forward, and he also may burn out in the process. You may strike people as solid and businesslike on first impression, but after the first few years people will look to you for new thinking. If it's not forthcoming, they'll find someone else who is moving ahead and leave you behind.

Breakpoint Strategy

Immersing yourself in your work is fine on occasion but not all of the time, particularly not the bad times, when work-centered people tend to project a disconcerting aura of desperation. Don't let yourself become bankrupt of resources and real friends, family, and faith outside the business world.

Breakpoint Signal 2

You find yourself thinking: "These good times can't last. I've got to make hay while there's still sun."

Breakpoint Forces

When you were working in the mainstream corporate world, you received regular performance reviews, raises, promotions, and feedback from your superiors. You were encouraged to take pride in good reviews; after all, if you didn't show satisfaction, you'd have insulted your superiors. On your own, of course, you have to give yourself your own emotional feedback and take praise and satisfaction where you find it.

You may be special, but, to repeat, you're still human. And the last time we looked, humans were still being produced with a basic need for reward and praise.

Breakpoint Strategy

Simplicity itself. Schedule a celebration with some ceremony when a goal is reached. The "ritual" may be nothing more time-consuming than a good lunch and the rest of the afternoon off on the day you put a big check in the bank. Find time to allow yourself to savor the moment without fretting about the next deal, loss of time, or where the next meal will come from.

PERSONAL BREAKPOINT 3: "THE WILLY LOMAN SYNDROME"

You find yourself thinking: "My customers are loyal because they know I'm a good person who is giving them their money's worth. I can count on them to stick with me."

Breakpoint Forces

We all remember how Willy Loman in *Death of a Salesman* fancied himself and his likable qualities to be the number-one concern of his customers. Would you spend more to give a better deal to Mr. Congeniality? Perhaps. Or perhaps not. It probably depends on the magnitude of the expense. Why expect your own customers to be any different?

Breakpoint Strategy

While congeniality is a plus, of course, base your business risks on hard practicalities and your good-guy image will be net extra.

Be *especially* wary of deluding yourself into thinking that personal loyalties to you will prompt potential customers to break ongoing relationships they've had with your competitors. Free market forces prompt managers to make business choices, no matter what they say about friendship. To ignore this hard reality is to set yourself up for financial pain and personal depression—the forces that made Willy Loman a tragedy instead of a success story.

POLITICAL BREAKPOINTS: "MY WAY OR THE HIGHWAY"

You became an entrepreneur because you had faith in yourself. You were probably less than ecstatic over corporate restrictions placed on your decision-making capability. So when you become "your own boss," you're fairly susceptible to a "my way or the highway" philosophy that too many entrepreneurs adopt.

Breakpoint Signal

You find yourself thinking: "It's my company, after all. I worked hard to get here. I'm not going to let anyone take it away from me, and for better or worse I'm going to rely on my own instincts and judgments."

Breakpoint Forces

This kind of attitude is okay if your idea of entrepreneurial activity is running a one-man hot-dog cart. If you're going to embark on an enterprise that's more substantial, however, you don't have the luxury of electing yourself dictator just because you sign the paychecks.

You may not meet too much resistance from those you hire if your autocratic attitude has been evident from the start. The odds are that you'll have attracted only yes-people or those who don't have ideas of their own.

All too many talented seconds-in-command are stifled by their "fearless leaders." The result is either less than optimal performance or an eventual defection, with resulting losses to number one.

I recall lunching with a former head of marketing for Timex Corporation. This individual, a very talented woman, was expressing her concern for the manner in which Fred Olsen, founder and entrepreneur, treated his people.

She felt that this fearless leader with all the resources one would need, made life so difficult for employees that attention was diverted away from the business at hand and toward themselves.

It frequently follows that those companies are also the ones with profit problems.

Contrast the Timex scenario with the Bic story, where people are highly regarded and motivated by Bruno Bic. Where Timex may be slowly drifting away, Bic is breaking records year after year.

Breakpoint Strategy

All mainstream corporate political rewards and punishments evolved for a reason: they fulfill basic human needs for recognition and growth. Be certain to provide employees with more opportunities to have ideas recognized. Be more like Bruno Bic—quick to let praise run off your back and onto those on whose shoulders you stand.

Save those moments of gloating over your own excellence for behind closed doors, if at all. Hearing someone sing "I did it my way" rarely motivates a subordinate. The excellent manager receives a real high from the success others realize on the job, whether or not the company is owned by that person.

SPECIAL POINTERS

As we've pointed out, the entrepreneur's initial major problem is generally cash flow. Here a woman may have a disadvantage despite special government agencies set up to help. Unfair and outdated as it may seem, much of the banking community has yet to free itself from a notion that a female entrepreneur may not be as "hungry" as a male, or is less goal-oriented, or, or, or—and that a loan to a woman's company may be somehow less desirable than a loan to a man's. Do not despair. The result is not necessarily that as a woman you won't get credit, but that you may find yourself with a loan that is two and a half points over prime, while your male counterpart and competition has a loan on more favorable terms.

Breakpoint Strategy

If you want to be taken seriously by lenders, your first step is to make use of the information we've provided above—and outdo your male counterparts by providing crisp, clear accounting and well-organized business plans. If this doesn't work, consider another bank—possibly a smaller institution where you'll be able to establish a relationship with someone with more clout.

As a second alternative, consider hiring a male accountant to attend banking presentations with you. His presence may have symbolic value.

As a last resort, consider a male "silent partner" as a guarantor. By sharing ownership, you may be able to attract someone who'll make your lender feel more secure. Remember, much of what we're discussing here is applicable in the start-up phase only. After you've gotten established with sound banking relations, differences would be minimal if there were any at all.

CHECKLIST FOR SPOUSES

Being the spouse of an entrepreneur has a lot to recommend it, especially if you the spouse are the primary breadwinner and you're comfortably well off and without debts. Your spouse's new business will be fun to talk about and can make for a stronger relationship as your spouse's success leads to increased self-confidence.

An old friend of mine I'll call Bob, who is a highly regarded insurance executive, has derived a good deal of fun and interest out of a new business undertaken by his wife, Mary, several years ago.

After working as a middle manager for a stuffy old ledger-manufacturing company, Mary decided to strike out on her own. With Bob's encouragement and a lump-sum settlement from her former employer, Mary and a partner bought a small paper-converting company. They struggled for a time.

During my last conversation with Bob, he told me that the business had grown steadily and profitably to such a degree that Mary was considering acquiring another firm to fill the gap in orders. And (lest women continue to smart over the preceding banking advice) the banks are calling to offer and aggressively pursue the new financing.

While Mary is as pleased and proud as can be with her new company, Bob is the one who talks it up. He's even mentioned early retirement a time or two.

On the other hand, this pattern is far from typical. Often the entrepreneur is the primary breadwinner and the spouse is treated to around-the-clock concern with work, plus the new uncertainty of knowing that there's no pension plan or excess profits in the fledgling company's program for another five years or so. Hand to mouth is the lifestyle, and it's a special spouse who thrives under these conditions.

Two tactics can make the road a bit easier. First, be sure in your own mind that your spouse is an entrepreneurial sort. Knowing that your spouse scored high in the entrepreneurial traits we've included in Chapter 5 can give you some comfort, since it's an indication that your spouse will fare better in this area than in the traditional corporate mainstream. Assuming that your spouse is of entrepreneurial blood, you can weather the almost inevitable hard times by recalling the success stories of Henry Ford, Colonel Sanders, and Ray Kroc (who founded McDonald's), among many others. All of these business titans failed on numerous attempts before they finally achieved spectacular success.

The other tactic we've found helpful to spouses of entrepreneurs is to resist a natural impulse to pitch in and help in the new "cottage company." Entrepreneurial types, you remember, want to make work-related decisions themselves. You can offer to help, of course, and many marital partnerships have been made immeasurably more beautiful by such teamwork—but be careful how you interfere with the fledgling CEO. Many will have a deep-seated need to get the new enterprise up and running independent of your help. Once they've proved their initial worth, they may welcome your aid.

Chapter 16

Chief Executive

Capsule Summary

After nearly two decades in the human resources field, we at Goodrich &
Sherwood have seen and heard more than our share about what makes a
good chief executive.

We've learned from chief executives themselves.

We've learned from their directors and their shareowners.

We've learned from their subordinate executives, of all ranks, at companies of every size from the biggest to the smallest.

We've learned from their *former* subordinates, too, many of whom
we've counseled individually or placed in CEO spots.

We've seen leadership styles come and go, into and out of fashion.
We've lived through success stories—and cautionary tales and disasters—
of many types, including:

—charismatic leaders who are known for inspiring and generating "creative ferment";

—more subdued, non-directive leaders whose lack of traits to "copycat"
leaves subordinates free to "be themselves" and "maximize their individual creativity";

—leaders sensitive to human relations who regularly pick up scraps of
discarded paper in the parking lots, slap backs in the employees' cafeteria,
and rub elbows on the company jogging trail, in the bowling alley, or on
the bench of the company softball diamond;

—close-to-the-vest imperial mystery men who stay ensconced in the corporate penthouse, devouring reports from all corners of their empires and issuing crisp, often cryptic directives without explanation;

—Patton-style flamboyant disciplinarians who will dress down a miscreant at the drop of a laurel-rimmed hat.

Through the seventies and eighties, we've counseled companies whose leaders fit these molds and more. We've even seen some organizations where there is *no* CEO and where the partners work on a collegial consensus-management system.

After this experience, we confidently assert two sweeping generalizations about CEO style:

—There are enough proponents of each style listed above to assure a continuous supply of success stories to recommend the strong points of each—particularly in good times.

—There are enough opponents of each style to assure a continuous supply of cautionary tales warning against the bad points of each—particularly in bad economic times.

You pays your money and you takes your choice. By the time you've reached CEO level, you should know which style is most comfortable for you. More important, you should know which subordinates work best with your particular style—and make your plans to hire and fire accordingly.

Different companies have different historical perspective, different futures, and operate under different economic conditions. No single leadership style will work all the time for every company. All have found it necessary to operate on a case-by-case basis rather than attempting to develop a single executive style.

However, lest it appear that we're advocates of the "whatever turns you on" or "whatever works" school, we do want to mention a few more points of consistency we have uncovered that may help you with the breakpoints you'll encounter as a CEO.

PERFORMANCE BREAKPOINT 1

Breakpoint Signals

Close your eyes and visualize the company five years from now. Generally, what do you see?

a. more of the same;
b. nothing;
c. you won't close your eyes and look ahead five years;
d. you see a vision you know is anathema to most of your board of directors and particularly to your chairman, who is the former CEO;
e. great success, in detail your subordinates wouldn't recognize.

Breakpoint Forces

Leaders are paid to lead. On those frequent occasions when people need to draw on inspiration beyond "the satisfaction of a job well done," they'll focus on their emotional need for a secure position in a company with a solid future. They look to you to help determine what that future will be.

In many cases the merits or shortcomings of your vision for the company's future don't matter. It's knowing that you have a vision, that you're planning to take the company into the next decade, that makes people willing to give their best performances.

Breakpoint Strategy

Just as you charted your own career path, you need your own private five-year, ten-year, and fifteen-year plan for the company.

The wider the range of input for the plan, the greater the chance for success. The narrower the audience for your presentation of the plan, the less the chance of failure. So avoid the publicizing of your plans by overeager subordinates, particularly until implementation is assured.

While the need for secrecy may sound Machiavellian, reality dictates that every company plan must be revised with the times. It's also true that no leader, not even you, is going to score 100 percent as a visionary. Although rational people understand this dynamic, watching their company make a 180-degree turn causes many people to doubt the leader's ability to manage. If the reverberations are strong enough, strong leadership can become reactive, fearing failure.

It goes without saying that as CEO you need a vision of the company's future in order to plan your own. Your retirement or job change will depend upon the opportunities you see coming in your present post, just as they did in the days when you were an executive in the lower ranks.

Avoid the mistake of adopting an unspoken attitude of those around you that you'll be on the job forever. After all, you wouldn't expect any of your subordinates to discuss your leaving, or even hint that the day might come when you could be replaced. However, that day *will* come, and it's up to you to recognize and plan for the best time for it to occur.

Don't wait, as some have, until you're asked to leave by employees or stockholders. The Werner/Heyman struggle at GAF is a classic example of a chairman who, having lost momentum and the support of a goodly chunk of former supporters, hung on until the company was forcibly wrested from him.

Only a sea captain plans to go down with the ship, and today most expect to take retirement and depart the navy far in advance of the ship's demise.

Several years ago at a luncheon for Marvin Bower, the insightful former head of McKinsey & Company, I was pleased to hear him say that long-term business growth was achieved by several direct management actions, two of which I recall were a vision that could allow those struggling in the trenches to buy into growth (a self-fulfilling objective) and the hiring of high-caliber people at all levels to deliver the vision.

PERFORMANCE BREAKPOINT 2

Another performance area where we've seen new CEOs frequently get into trouble is in the public relations/advertising end of the business. Particularly if the background of the new chief is in accounting or production where public contact has been limited, there seems to be trauma attached to the thought of one's words or images reaching tens of millions of people. As a novice, you may be self-conscious and hesitant until you become used to the process and accept the symbolic mantle of leadership you bear. You may try to "prove a point"—and ignore the realistic appraisals of your PR staff. Caution and conservatism are key at this point. Don't say anything you'd not care to have repeated, and be clear when you do communicate so that your message is delivered intact.

Breakpoint Strategy

The perils of uncertain public relations were illustrated by an incident that occurred some time ago. Fred Olsen, at that time chairman of Timex Corporation, whom I've mentioned previously, became very upset and terminated an executive over a disagreement the two had involving a public relations action on a new product Timex was planning to launch.

Olsen was reportedly enraged that a public reference to the product was made—even after the industry had known that the introduction was forthcoming.

Our advice is to treat public relations and advertising professionals in the same manner you treat and manage other professionals. Ask questions that tie in with your vision and further your goals, questions about what they're doing and why—the research evidence they've amassed as backup and the alternatives they can propose.

Don't make the mistake of letting it be known that you're approving a campaign because your wife was favorably impressed, as I recall Charles Revson of Revlon fame did a number of years ago. After all, your wife isn't a typical consumer and a decision to move ahead or not should not be perceived as whimsical.

Additional note: You may be tempted to give your spouse the job of decorating the new office suite. Some executives, usually in smaller companies, bring in their wives to reign as ladies of the manor in matters of decor and architecture. Such feudal behavior rarely is well received and frequently leads to resentment.

PERSONAL BREAKPOINT 1

If you've risen in the mainstream corporate world, you probably aren't as susceptible to the autocrat's pitfalls as your entrepreneurial counterpart.

Nonetheless, you might do well to glance over that material in the preceding chapter and take a few fleeting moments to reflect on the virtues of team play and man's basic nature as a social animal.

Your most difficult personal breakpoint, however, is likely to take one of two forms: either you'll experience what we at G&S call the "top-of-the-ladder syndrome" and lose your balance; or you'll experience the "sands-of-time complex" and be tempted to overstay your welcome.

Breakpoint Signal: "Top-of-the-Ladder Syndrome"

You close your eyes and try to picture your office five years from now and see:

a. someone else in your chair;
b. nothing, because you're afraid to close your eyes lest one of your subordinates think you're sleeping on the job.

Breakpoint Forces

You have reached the top of the ladder, and to get there you've concentrated and learned your climbing lessons very well. You may have learned so well, in fact, that climbing is now an ingrained part of your lifestyle.

If you're climbing a ladder as high as the ladder extends, you know what eventually happens. You wind up standing on the top rung, where your balance is unsteady, and you're forced to think more about the ladder itself than what to do now that you've arrived.

Breakpoint Strategy

A common top executive weakness we hear about year after year involves behavior modification upon reaching the top. Suddenly you've arrived. No need to fight windmills, so you slow down and focus your attention on the corporate vision and on trouble spots in the company.

It is the talented top exec who realizes that the same vigor is not necessary to emphasize a point that was necessary when at the VP level or below.

Modify your reaction. Recognize that a rippling effect is created whenever you speak. Devote your chase, capture, and kill attention to goals elsewhere, perhaps outside the firm on boards or association work.

If the organization needs your top-gun attributes, you'll be called upon. In the meantime, you'll elicit better information from your people if they know that you're controlled and won't gun them down at the first glimmer of a problem.

Don't allow yourself to be overly concerned with holding your position. Instead, immerse yourself in what your customers, suppliers, bankers, and especially the investing public thinks of the company. Establish, change, or reinforce your corporate culture. Then communicate this information to your employees and to your board of directors. Encourage the board of directors to participate in what you've learned, your observations, and what you propose to change.

By maintaining continuous focus on what the company's doing and where it's headed *outside* its doors, you'll fulfill your duties as leader. If you allow yourself to be focused on keeping ahead of those around you—balancing on the ladder—you'll not stay too long at the top.

PERSONAL BREAKPOINT 2

It's a familiar theme in literature and life. We each have limited time on this planet, and only so much can be accomplished. On the other hand, the farther up the ladder we progress, the more opportunities for accomplishment we can see. Put both these traits together in a CEO, and you have what we call a "sands-of-time complex." Sooner or later, the CEO probably becomes legacy-conscious, the equivalent of a President whose mind is on what the historians will say rather than what's best for the country.

Breakpoint Signal: "The Sands of Time"

You find yourself ending each day thinking not of what you've completed but of how many things were left undone.

You develop a sudden urge to relocate the company headquarters and construct a new central office building or "campus."

Your instincts tell you to expand, even when all the objective business market signals tell you it's time to pull in your horns and lie low.

Like a furtive desire to flip to the obituary pages before you scan the business news, these signals are intimations of your own mortality and the wish that 'tweren't so. If you let these signals interfere with your business judgment, you'll lose your chance of being remembered favorably.

Breakpoint Strategy

Focus on doing what you can do and what can be done, as though today were your last in office and you had handpicked your successor. Don't allow a sense of time slipping away to color your emotional outlook, since this will be quickly transmitted to your subordinates, who generally expect to be around longer than you. If you try to communicate your sense of urgency to them, they won't share it and are likely to misinterpret a "time is fleeting" approach as an indication that a real disaster is impending for the company.

Your anxieties about the shortage of days remaining may be exacerbated by physical ailments. Now, we're aware that after nearly two decades of a fitness craze in America, you may have developed a resistance to being preached to by exercise addicts. We're not about to exhort you to start a jogging program here and now. But you should be aware that fitness can be a strong factor in prolonging your productive years and in maximizing your efficiency. It also serves as a good symbolic touch to let the rest of the company, and your directors, know that you're able to keep a firm hand on the tiller. Many of the country's finest CEOs are among the most fit for their age in the United States. Our President is a prime example.

POLITICAL BREAKPOINT 1: IMAGE PROBLEMS

Breakpoint Signals

1. Be aware of the symbolism involved in your day-to-day actions. Whatever makes a "good picture" can be picked up and made a part of your "image" by people who want to follow a "colorful" leader.

We have no bromides to offer regarding what trappings will enhance your image in the most appealing manner. However, we can say with some certainty that your "honeymoon" period will end much sooner than expected if you consciously adopt your predecessor's visual mannerisms. Whether you've liked them, admired them, emulated them, or even idolized them, don't show them to your public now. Employees need to know that you're your own person.

One newly appointed CEO we know of effectively enhanced his "honeymoon" period with visual reinforcement. He had lunch with the regional managers of each territory—some fifty individuals per region—just after being helicoptered around the region's borders accompanied by the general manager. The "big picture" view of the territory was then made the subject of the day's luncheon discussion.

2. Your first firing. No president expects a term as CEO without having to make this difficult move. Our own survey data and others indicate that terminating a close subordinate is the most stressful career event for any executive, and you're not likely to be an exception to this general rule. However, your job lies not only in severing relations where and when appropriate but in projecting a proper businesslike

attitude regarding the circumstances and the executive to those remaining.

Your first firing may be a purge of those who opposed your ascending to the top spot. Make it easy for them to leave by helping them to find other positions outside the company, and by generating offers if possible.

POLITICAL BREAKPOINT 2: "THE USURPER"

You need strong officers to run various divisions of your company, and you know that the ambitions of many will include a shot at the top spot. Those who don't want to be number two will naturally be looking to unseat you—despite protestations of loyalty. It's basic human nature that's been around since well before Caesar and isn't likely to change. The common perception is that if you're at a higher level, you have a better job.

Breakpoint Signals

Watch for shifts in *symbolic* leadership—the aspects of company culture that relate to personal style. In your hands, if you have the leadership of the company, is unstated power to influence these mannerisms. Your dress, your car, the phrases and metaphors you use, and your hobbies all will find favor and imitators if your constituents are loyal—as a number of jelly-bean manufacturers discovered to their delight after President Reagan took office.

The signal that there's a problem comes when you notice a group of subordinates with similar styles that are different from yours. When you identify the top-ranking subordinate—usually an officer in the company— whose style they're mimicking, you've found your potential rival.

Be especially attentive if the change in style is something other than personal or corporate culture. A strategic change in business policy—a sixty-day time period to cure contract defaults rather than ninety days, for example—can be passed off by a rival as a matter of personal business judgment. To oppose it may seem petty. But this kind of a change is a change in company policy, and that's a direct challenge to your prerogative.

Breakpoint Forces

People often act out of self-interest. If they're following a rival on a different track, it is usually because that person is providing leadership, charisma, or something that you're not. You can identify the "something" and, using the leverage of your position, you can provide it in a bigger, better, or more effective way. You can also, leveraging your power of office, isolate your rival and send the appropriate signal to the potential usurper and to the rest of the company. For instance, the head of a Fortune 500 company I know sent a rival to run the international division for the company. So much time in an airplane traveling from place to place was required that the problem was solved.

Breakpoint Strategy

About a year ago I was on a hunting trip in Maryland with the president of a major national realty company, whom I'll call Brian. With us was one of his vice-presidents. During the trip Brian made frequent reference to this VP in his presence and talked about his heir-apparent status and promotion in the not too distant future.

After we had been together for a day or two, the VP loosened up and late one night after a few extra scotches suggested that he could do a better job than Brian, etc., etc. I thought it odd to take this stance when he had Brian's support and encouragement.

Obviously, the ingredient at work here was a form of unchecked aggression. The lack of patience expressed to me was also being transmitted throughout the division. The eventual result was that Brian had to reverse his posture, demoting the executive and ultimately terminating him.

Once you've identified a rival, carefully evaluate points of difference between your styles. Then take a look at some other aspect of your style that will help you reestablish leadership in your company—and be certain that you don't embarrass yourself in the process by choosing a point of style that isn't really your own.

One CEO we know had an unfortunate experience when he made this mistake. He sensed he was losing allegiance to a rival whose weekend camping and mountain-climbing excursions had attracted a number of senior-level emulators. He felt left out and had no interest in camping. So he took up jogging. After a few months, to publicize his success, he set up a company-sponsored five-kilometer road race, which he entered with a pledge to "go for a personal best." He encouraged all employees to enter and the response was gratifying. Unaccustomed to racing, he started out too fast, did not pace himself, and dropped out halfway through the race complaining of chest pains. I didn't have the nerve to ask if his hardy mountain-climbing rival won the race.

Finally, if you find your styles incompatible, isolate your rival and center your power. We prefer a direct approach with the individual where concerns and alternatives are discussed openly. If, however, a more subtle course correction is desirable, you can send a signal that's unmistakable—for example, by holding a meeting at your home to discuss a matter important to the company's future. Schedule the first of these meetings for a time when your rival is out of town or immersed in another key activity. Then when there are subsequent meetings on the same subject, you won't need to make the same face-saving schedule adjustment.

A more direct technique to isolate a rival is the "personal assignment for the president." You can send the rival on a traveling and consulting mission. We've seen many of these, and, in larger companies, we've even seen special positions created at higher pay to keep the potential usurper away from the corridors of power.

The message soon gets through.

What we've just described, as you no doubt have surmised, is the worst-case scenario with a valued employee. The ideal approach, of course, is to harness the valuable qualities inherent in a strong executive and, to use a riding term, stay in direct contact with your horse.

Most often when a CEO loses control to a rival it's due to losing interest in the company, the job, or the people, or the stockholders. At some point along the way, something slipped. It is your responsibility as CEO to surround yourself with people who will monitor the pulse of the organization and keep you informed on issues like employee morale, turnover, stockholder concern, etc.

By keeping direct contact with your key people, you'll see and channel aggressive tendencies long before a confrontation occurs. Remember, as in sighting a gun, small corrections are best. Keep the organization on track. The more radical the change, the more difficult the adjustment for the organization. Ideally, you should use all the talents a rival has to offer and concentrate your effort on positive management technique.

Remember, your power ultimately lies with your board of directors and controlling stockholders. Perception is fact. To maintain their support, work hard to see that the company performance satisfies their criteria and see that their various other needs are met, giving them the status and the relationship they want and deserve.

A word about the board.

When you join a new company where the chairman and board are in place, the operating environment you'll enter will be very different from that of a company where you manage, direct, change, and build the board yourself.

At a company with a chairman over an existing board, you may find that you are in title CEO but in actual practice functioning as an EVP while the chairman and board make the decisions.

Take this into careful consideration as you negotiate and evaluate your offer with an eye toward "real" control versus title-only power.

Many of the nation's larger companies create division presidents who report to an executive committee headed by the chairman, or by the president, chairman, and board. While these companies vary greatly in the range of autonomy allowed for division presidents, final decisions, particularly those involving policy, are made above.

A CHANCE TO MOVE

The CEO's job is more volatile than most other executive positions, according to data developed over the past ten years.

As you keep your information network active in gathering data for day-to-day operations or evaluating the effect they're having on the company, also develop your own initial campaign to keep your name and your accomplishments in the minds of those with whom you have contact. You can expect offers from larger corporations and smaller; from those whose CEOs are actually retiring to companies desperate for a "savior" or magician to undo knots of confusion left by a disgraced predecessor.

Evaluate each of these moves in the same way you've evaluated other positions with your checklist from Chapter 6. The most significant difference between evaluating a prospective presidency and evaluating a prospective middle-management position lies in the interview process. In interviewing for a presidency, you can ask more targeted questions since much of the data on the company is public. Since you won't have much time to spend discussing the parameters of your job description, you can target on broad issues like how the chairman and board view the needs for the future.

We're often asked if a CEO from a small or medium-sized company can find happiness as an EVP at a major corporation. Our answer is a definite maybe, if the job is a meaningful line position and the person hired is to be groomed for the top slot.

Take ample time to review financial planning and tax matters with your attorney or financial planner prior to accepting any offer and give your experts enough time to do a thorough analysis. The days of the "golden parachute" may be waning, but you owe it to yourself to cut the best deal you can initially—who knows what the future may bring? Perhaps you'll come out on the short end of a merger or takeover.

As you approach the interview, remember that corporate culture is key. You as chief must be satisfied with your "business family"; if not, you'll either have to live with things as they are or change them.

Change is often necessary and sometimes it takes a real punch to wake people up. Jack Welsh of GE said in an interview recently, "Sometimes I want to shake people and tell them things have changed." Colonel Sanders sued Heublein to get the changes he wanted accomplished, and Lee Iacocca turned Chrysler upside down to produce a quality product.

Make certain as you evaluate the company that you've adequately evaluated the negatives. All the negatives. Remember, it's not one of the 432 positives that will cause you to fail. It well may be one of the three negatives you ignored when considering the overwhelming data in support of the move.

If I had to identify any one area where CEOs have failed by changing companies, it's here. They're so accustomed to being in control that they don't read the sands properly. The cavalry had an old expression. You never see the arrow that gets you in the neck.

So devote ample time to your failure analysis and cover yourself carefully on these points in your contract.

Chapter 17

Advisory Power

Capsule Summary

You've set aside the day-to-day cares of being a chief executive, but you retain a substantial ownership position in your company.

You've become the power behind the throne. As chairman of the board, you spend an average of two hours a day reading reports from your company's industry and the rest of the time making contacts with other industry leaders on the golf course, in the hunting camp, or at the club.

Once a month there's a board meeting where you preside. It seems that your experience is all coming into play at these meetings as the problems of the company fall into the same familiar patterns you once encountered so frequently. You keep these meetings brief and focused on the company's long-range goals. Fortunately, there is a consensus on where the company is headed, so the meetings generally go smoothly.

The chief executive you've appointed phones you once in a while to ask your advice when an emergency comes up. Fortunately, the emergencies are generally predictable and represent problems you've faced before.

If these scenarios sound too good to be true, it's because they are. These are visions of life as an adviser that we'd all like to have. But from King Lear to Winston Churchill in the political world, and throughout the modern business world, the mantle of leadership is never passed easily. At G&S, we've worked with the advisers of many companies and can state with absolute authority that though the adviser's path is less mazelike than a chief executive's, it's nonetheless a bumpy road.

Understanding the dynamics of the advisory relationship with your company is key to negotiating your way past major pitfalls and potholes.

Breakpoint Signal: Phase I: Letting Go

Nick and Maurice had built the Johnson Construction Company from ground zero to its present personal position as one of the top ten in the state. Each of the two partners had assets of more than ten million dollars, and the company was recognized as a leader in both commercial and government construction. The partners each had sons, who were active in the business and had learned not only the difficult job of estimating but the more difficult art of negotiating with subcontractors and developers.

Both partners were looking forward to turning the business over to their sons. The transition was set, with a "retirement" ceremony scheduled.

Three months before the "retirement," Nick died.

Maurice maintained a brave and resolute exterior throughout the sadness of the months that followed. He kept to the "retirement" schedule because "Nick would have wanted it that way."

However, during the months that followed "retirement," Maurice found himself unable to let go of the reins. He would wake up in the morning with an urge to call in and find out what was happening with each new project. He would "stop by" about eleven o'clock at the office and stay usually till three or four in the afternoon.

When subcontractors or owners called in and asked for him, he took the calls. Then, in casual conversations with either of the two "boys," he'd refer to the information he'd picked up during the day and ask how they planned to respond.

About six months after this "retirement," Maurice got a call from a bonding company about a seven-million-dollar office building project in an "inner-city enterprise zone." Maurice's son had signed the application and committed the company's assets. The bonding company's officer explained that the bonding company wanted Maurice's personal guarantee as well.

Maurice was stunned. He hadn't even heard of the project. The company had always steered away from inner-city construction. With all the added risks involved, Nick and Maurice had always felt it wasn't worth the additional time and energy.

When he confronted the "boys" about the new project, he got another shock. They each faced him down with cold indifference. "We thought about it," Maurice's son said, "and it's what we want to do. That's it. If you don't agree, you can fire us. After all, you're the majority shareholder."

Breakpoint Forces

Maurice had been working as a partner for twenty-five years, sharing the responsibilities and authority of the company's top management. In the three-month interim between Nick's death and Maurice's "retirement," he got a taste of what full authority felt like. Even though he was unwilling to admit it in the emotional turmoil of the bereavement and even though he went through with his "retirement" because "Nick would have wanted it that way," Maurice was unwilling to let go. He had his own vision of the company—admittedly, a vision reflecting the status quo —and he didn't really want to delegate the operational authority.

As a result, he lost his advisory power.

Breakpoint Strategy

Examine your own motives. First, recognize that you'll enjoy maintaining your influence over company affairs. Your status among many of your contacts outside the company may depend upon maintaining that influence. The subcontractors and owners—the major customers, clients, and suppliers you've dealt with—won't stop calling you just because you officially announce that you have moved out of the executive suite. The congratulatory calls and the calls "just to keep in touch" will continue and substantive business matters will find their way into these talks. Not only is the force of habit strong; you are also now an influential lobbyist who can speak on their behalf to the company management.

Be quick to refer any substantive points to your successor, not just by talking about what you've learned when you "touch base" but also when you speak to the outside party. Make it clear that you're not functioning either as an intermediary or as the decision maker, however tempting both those roles may seem.

The penalty for yielding to either of these temptations is twofold. You interfere with the company's operation and drive your successor to an opposing position. Rather than concentrating on what's best for the company, your successor tries to assert authority independent of you—which means taking the path opposing your recommendations, regardless of whether your recommendations are right or wrong. Assuming that you have good advice to give the company, this means that your advice will be wasted.

The other penalty you pay is an inevitable falling-out between you and your successor. Either you will back down and "lose," or your successor will back down and you will lose again—since the successor you picked has not made the grade. You may have to start over, either as chief executive or with a new chief executive. And the same problems will be repeated.

Breakpoint Signal: Phase II: "Resistance Testing"

In any advisory situation, you can expect resistance testing. It will take one of two forms. Either you'll test your successor or your successor will test you.

A few years ago I received a call from the chairman of a large company located in Pittsburgh. He asked me about possibilities I might be aware of on boards in the United States. He said that he had finally made the decision to step down after seeing how his protégé handled several crisis situations, one of which he had set up.

He said he finally was convinced that everything was under control and he felt comfortable putting time in elsewhere.

Business in the United States has traditionally adopted a "prove it" attitude toward companies getting started, turnarounds, and new management. It is the "prove it" approach that drives business and management today. Ask Lee Iacocca, or perhaps John DeLorean: "proving it" is powerful medicine.

Breakpoint Forces

Each party needs to know who's in charge. The company operates on a hierarchical basis, and leadership flows best from the position that's symbolically at the head. On a political level, no one likes to think that the President is looking to his predecessor for direction. The same applies to business. Nonetheless, your advisory power, if it's to be exercised, means that you don't simply "say your piece and let the devil take the hindmost."

Breakpoint Strategy

Remember, your advisory power lies in the experience you've had and in your ability to remain aloof from day-to-day operations. When your advice is challenged, focus on the long-range goals that you know are agreed on, and repeat that you don't see how the action your successor is proposing will take the company in that direction.

Avoid recommendation of specific actions. That's the business of your successor. When asked for specific recommendations in a given situation, you can recount experiences you've had, but be sure you recount them as data your successor can consider rather than specific orders to fall in lockstep behind the past. It's easy enough to make this distinction with a remark or two such as "Maybe this will help," or "Maybe things have changed—you know more about that than I."

Breakpoint Signal: Phase III: "Adviser to Observer"

Not everyone's cut out for the advisory role, and not everyone can stay in it over a long period of time. Here are some signals we've found that indicate you should let go from your advisory powers and move to an observer's position.

1. You find that the day-to-day problems of the company rather than its long-range goals are what really interest you.
2. You find that your influence at the company is waning. People don't seek out your advice the way they used to.
3. You find that you are not keeping up with changes in your industry or your field. You leave that sort of thing for the "younger generation."

Even though your health and energy levels may be high, any of the above signals should prompt you to consider seriously letting go and moving to an observer's position. Why? Because all three indicate you're out of sync with the needs of your company.

The first and third signals indicate that you want to be back in your former job and that you aren't interested in providing the broader view the company needs for its future.

The second signal indicates that the company isn't receptive to what you're offering. You can't force them to listen, unless you own a majority share. And even if you could lay down the law, what good would it do? The effect would be temporary at best.

Know when to go gracefully. Paradoxically, you may find that stepping down from a formally held advisory position opens up new informal contacts with company management or board members, and that you'll have a more receptive audience for your ideas when people don't feel obligated to listen.

Chapter 18

Retirement

The Story Continues

Capsule Summary

Note: You should read this chapter if you're ten years or less from the earliest day you might consider retiring.

You may wonder why we include a chapter about retirement in a book about careers. After all, you might think, a career is one thing, retirement is a whole different ball game. And you'd be right.

But in today's economy, the two life stages are often intermingled. People will retire from one position and work part-time in another, or they'll continue in a "retirement mode" but save for capital investment that will give them the "family business" they've been dreaming about for years, or they will make a career of managing the assets they have accumulated over a lifetime.

The point to remember is that because retirement is a whole different career, you'll come into it as a trainee. There are, of course, some often warned-of pitfalls that you may have thought about, but there are others we've seen at G&S in our counseling of early retirees.

These pitfalls occur not only in your personal life but also in the new "political" bonds you'll need to form.

The key to negotiating your way and to acclimatizing yourself to the new world of retirement is through early preparation. If you're within ten years of the earliest date you might consider retiring, read on.

PERFORMANCE BREAKPOINTS

Who's judging your performance?

When you retire, you find that you're the boss at last and that there is no good reason to set the alarm to go off any earlier than you'd wake up on a holiday. You may look forward to "just fishing" or "just shopping," or taking time to enjoy the little things—all the clichés that are bandied about to make retirement seem like the dessert that comes as a reward for all those working years. We hope to convince you that this may not be the right approach for most people, particularly those who have retired early with few hobbies or interests.

Your performance goals are measured not only by your own internal sense of self-worth and satisfaction but also by your loved ones who depend upon you. They're simple enough. You might consider retirement the ultimate "steady path."

You want to keep your income stream constant and secure.

You want to maintain a comfortable living standard.

You want to do what's important for you and your loved ones.

You want to maintain your health.

Regrettably, there are any number of ways you can foul up on meeting these performance objectives. Here's one of the most common.

Breakpoint Signals

Annie reached retirement age just two years after her husband, Jack. One of her company's first mid-level managers, Annie had always wanted to own her own business. When the chance came to buy a small yarn shop in her town's central shopping district, Annie leaped at the opportunity. She had always enjoyed knitting, she'd become familiar with the ads of major distributors she'd seen in knitting magazines, she knew yarn types, needle sizes, patterns, instructions—it seemed like a natural.

Adding to the plus column of the decision was her husband's business experience. While Annie had been in production, Jack had been in accounting in his company. The balance sheets and tax returns would be duck soup for him, she reasoned.

As soon as she and Jack agreed, they gutted each of their IRAs, pledged their stocks, and mortgaged the family home to buy the yarn shop.

What neither had counted on was the time and energy a small business demands—particularly a small retail business. Annie hadn't become accustomed to dealing with the public during her work career, and neither had her husband. Remaining pleasant while training a subordinate had come naturally to Annie—after all, she knew the subordinate could do good work and she was committed to getting a future return for the company on its training investment. However, it didn't seem quite as natural to Annie to stifle her indignation when an ill-tempered customer became insulting or unreasonable. Shoplifters and "browsers" who pawed through displays without buying began to get under Annie's skin.

But she and Jack were in too deep to back away. The business, upsetting to Annie or not, demanded attention from nine to five. Profits weren't high enough to afford to hire someone to mind the store. So nine to five six days a week was taken up within the store's four walls. Also, to boost sales, Annie gave knitting lessons evenings at adult education classes at the local high school two nights a week.

One day she looked at Jack over breakfast coffee, and everything seemed to come down on her at once. "I burst into tears," she recalls. "The dream I'd jumped into so eagerly turned out to be a terrible ball and chain. I don't know what I'd have done if Jack hadn't been so understanding."

Annie was lucky. She came to her realization during an expansion period of the economy, when retail sales in her town were up nearly 30 percent over the previous year. Through her landlord she was able to find another tenant, a jeweler, who took over her lease at an increased rent, which gave Annie enough profit to make the payments on her purchase of the business after liquidating the inventory. Though their IRAs were gone, Annie and Jack were able to walk away from this mistake with their stock and family home intact.

Breakpoint Forces

The twenty to forty years you spend in the work force can give you more than just "business experience." So many years of being a subordinate can build up an overpowering urge to "be your own boss," run your own business, take risks, go for it. With 600,000 new businesses opening up each year, they seem to have become part of our national ideal, with the entrepreneur now touted as exemplifying the American spirit in a way the organization-oriented manager doesn't.

Breakpoint Strategy

Hindsight is always 20/20, but you can maximize the odds on the success of your own business as a retiree if you adopt the same healthy skepticism toward buying a business you'd naturally have toward a vendor who wanted to sell you a retirement home in a retirement community three thousand miles from your present home. The thought of picking up and moving to a new world is enough to set your emotional brakes and make you automatically dream up a few worst-case scenarios. If you do the same for taking on a business of your own, you'll at least forestall the foreseeable drawbacks to the "business" move.

Using the worst-case scenario, think of your cash-flow goals and how the income stream from your new business will fit in to keep you at or better than your present level.

Project the future market.

Examine your experience in *all* the facets of the business that you'll have to work with.

Determine your ability to hire a manager or other employees to give you the freedom you'd like to have.

A key consideration at this point is whether the business could ever stand alone. If you're putting in a great deal of time and effort, do you want a business hobby or a significant income generator?

Hobby businesses tend to be those restricted by store size, where significant effort is expended for often minimal financial results. Ask yourself, after a twenty-minute sale when it closes, how much do you make? If you find that you need a constant stream of customers in the yarn shop to break even, you've got an idea how profitable your business will be.

You'll need to sell a good deal of yarn just to pay operating expenses.

On the other hand, selling one Duncan Phyfe chair may make your month. Examples of hobby businesses are craft shops, small specialized-food stores, snack-food stores, bait shops, card shops, and do-it-yourself businesses. Remember, if the price of your product is low, you'll need high-volume sales. High price, low volume. This is significant when you calculate the cost of labor and your time.

You might also consider being a "not too silent" partner in a business. Here you can provide capital and your partner provides much of the expertise and the labor, and you share profits. If you can structure your investment this way, usually with a younger and hungrier "active" partner, you may meet more of your goals than if you try to go it alone or with your husband or wife.

PERSONAL BREAKPOINTS

We've all heard the stories about people retiring, moving to Florida, and dying within six months.

The bored and listless retiree is, regrettably, familiar to many of us. Mornings spent in bed or watching game shows, eating toast and tea because it's "too much trouble" to fix a real meal, a listless turn or two around the shopping mall and a chat on the courthouse steps or park bench with other kindred bored spirits. Visits to the doctor. Complaints of fatigue and listlessness. Antidepressant medication. Hoped-for improvement doesn't materialize and the doctor urges, "Get out and do more. Be active."

And the unhappy retiree asks in all seriousness, "Do more of what?"

At G&S we've found, through follow-up programs with former clients, that personal breakpoints during the retirement years are unavoidable. We list four major forces that are most likely to throw you into the doldrums. Two you can do something about, and the other two are merely questions of personal philosophy more than career planning. However, we include them since we've found them to be among the most significant, on the theory that forewarned is forearmed.

Breakpoint Signal 1

At retirement age, you are probably witnessing your own children's first real struggles over the long haul. By now some of them may be through the rookie and Young Turk phases of their careers, so that the problems that were once concealed by general hope and expectancy during a "new" period are no longer hidden to your insightful view. At this age, your children may be repeating some of the mistakes you wish you'd avoided— despite all your advice to the contrary—and may also be going through personal traumas such as divorce, separation from children, and so on. These problems hit seniors harder than they hit their children, for two reasons. First, because you're older and your energy and resistance levels aren't as high as they once were. Second, because you're on the sidelines and can do little to help; your emotion can't vent itself in constructive action.

Breakpoint Strategy

It's a matter of personal philosophy as much as anything else, but one truth seems self-evident. Although your children are very precious to you, you can make yourself miserable by trying to view them as your "achievement." Their lives are their own, and your suffering vicariously for them doesn't help make their road any easier to travel. Maintaining a discreet distance may be the best policy for both sides.

Breakpoint Signal 2

When you move to a retirement community or to the Sunbelt or wherever, you add loneliness and isolation to the new world of retirement. Of course, you make new friends—but the newly formed relationships may not provide what the old relationships did. And cutting off your geographical and neighborhood ties—at the same time you're severing your work relationships—can create a stress overload.

Breakpoint Strategy

Ask yourself just how important warm winters are for you before you begin planning a radical retirement move. Also, consider the *quality* of the relationships you'll be maintaining and forming during the years *prior* to the move. If you're looking forward to the day when you'll leave your community, or even if you're not looking forward to it but just know that it's coming, you may unconsciously distance yourself from those around you. Getting out of the habit of forming close relationships can impoverish the working years before you move, and can make the years following your move more difficult to adjust to.

Breakpoint Signal 3

Whose goals are these anyway?

The third major personal problem area we find is work-related. People who've occupied management or sales positions are prone to adopt a "company goal" attitude. Salespersons represent their company to others. When they retire, whom do they represent? The manager works hard to implement company policy. When retired, what is there to implement? The goal-vacuum phenomenon is aggravated by a related retirement misconception, the "golden years" or "retirement as dessert" point of view. When you're convinced that your retirement years are the "goodies" that you've earned for your working career, you can be headed for disappointment. The reality is that, in the rewards category, nothing really changes before or after retirement. You have a stream of income without direct work, it's true, but in actuality most of the rewards you were getting before you retired were not connected with money. The rewards were related to achievements you made, problems you solved, help for others, and the status you gained for yourself.

When you retire, none of those reward needs have changed. All that's changed is your source of income. While income no longer comes from your daily employment activities, all the other rewards you've become accustomed to—and need as a human being—still come from working.

Breakpoint Strategy

Work during retirement should be directed toward the goals you set before retirement. Meeting these goals is where you'll get your satisfaction. The type of goal we're referring to is not a trip to the Pyramids or the Taj Mahal, though such trips may be a fond dream or travel objective for next year. We're talking about achievement-related goals rather than reward goals. If you've been keeping up your career chart, and are familiar with the kinds of activities you like, give you the greatest satisfaction, and you perform best, you'll already have your list prepared (if not, just turn to the "Test Yourself" chapter and start there).

Your goal is to apply these activities to projects that your value sense tells you are worthwhile. Perhaps you're directing yourself toward entrepreneurial tasks to build a second fortune, or you may be doing volunteer work for a cause you believe in. Either way, the goals you set are your ticket away from a potential slough of despond.

By viewing your retirement years as a continuing work process, you avoid the potential trap of the "bored vacationer" and maintain self-esteem.

Your personal health is the fourth key to maximizing chances for success—whether you're working for a living or not. The data are overwhelming in support of exercise and a prudent diet, both of which we recommend as a fundamental part of your retirement goal program. Check with your doctor before you begin, of course, but if your doctor tells you not to exercise, we strongly recommend you get a second opinion. After all, exercise can range from running or walking to isometrics, where little physical movement is required.

POLITICAL BREAKPOINTS

Your retirement plans may focus on solitary activity as your key "production" goal, but whether you're looking to spend your time woodworking, beekeeping, or apple farming, you'll profit from a network.

After retirement, of course, your network won't be used to move you up the career ladder. Instead, your network will assist you in maintaining advisory power by providing new perspectives for your advice and new outlets for your energies.

Breakpoint Signals

When you were working, you were perhaps adept at picking up political signals. If your name was omitted from a circulating memo, if you weren't asked to a meeting, if you weren't copied on a letter, if you noticed people weren't coming into your office as frequently as before, you took steps to change the situation or identify a new one. You were moved by economic necessity—and so were your peers.

The same signals apply upon retirement. While you don't have regularly structured paperwork or meetings in which these signals manifest themselves on a daily basis, on a weekly basis—at club meetings, at church gatherings, or in telephone contacts—you'll pick up the same signals.

The danger during retirement years is that isolation is an easier trap to fall into.

Many people handle isolation by establishing an active social or family network that perhaps they could maintain while they worked. This network is an extremely good means of avoiding or managing isolation.

Breakpoint Forces

Having retired, you may be naturally inclined to separate yourself from people who are still working. "They're too busy" or "They don't understand how I feel" can come all too easily to your mind when someone who's still working for a living forgets to make contact on a project of yours.

Don't let yourself fall into this trap. Maybe the working person is too busy—today—to make the contact. So what? If you were still working, you wouldn't have thought twice. You would have called the next day—and the next—until you made contact. That was your job. You were driven by necessity.

Now you're not. This lack of an economic spur can make it easy to slack off and, of course, it becomes doubly easy for the person who's still working to grow out of touch.

Do not let this happen. It's no excuse and it needn't be. You have the time and the energy to pursue the contact. It may require your developing a tougher hide to shun any impulse toward self-pity.

Breakpoint Strategy

If you *can* bring together the economic forces working for you in maintaining your network, so much the better.

You needn't be a majority stockholder to have some economic clout. People are motivated by self-interest, and self-interest is far broader than simple dollars and cents.

Professional salespeople and managers have acquired ways to appeal to one's self-interest without using money. These techniques are familiar to all of us, though we don't always put them into practice enough. Take time to consider what the other person wants *apart* from whatever project it is that may be the reason for your contact. Discuss those things that you know are important to the other person and learn what information that person needs. Then help find the information. Or perhaps the other person's interest may simply be a need for an objective ear—a good listener who can sympathize or admonish at the right moment.

Any good salesperson learns during working years that you've got to sell yourself *first* to someone who doesn't know you. If all a person learns about you when you first shake hands is that you're retired, the odds are you won't have elicited interest. Develop the habit of having a "one-minute presentation" about your current project or interest on the tip of your tongue. You'll elicit the interest of those you meet, and you'll feel more "current" as well.

A major aid in maintaining your retirement network is to have begun building it during your working years. Avoid the temptation during those last few years to concentrate too fully on your job. You can delude yourself into thinking you're being benefited by raising your salary to raise your pension, and you may be tempted to "go out in a blaze of glory," but this kind of thinking is shortsighted at best.

Remember, you're not "going out." You'll still wake up the next morning and be in your own bed with a day's worth of projects to work on. The only difference is that you won't be directly compensated.

So build that project list while you're still working. Form your network of kindred spirits and enthusiasts. This network will pay big dividends as you cultivate and nurture it for as long as these projects continue to hold your interest.

When you've retired, the best way to assert your independence is to start managing your career.